From Applicant to Hired

Unlocking the Secrets of Resumes, Interviews, and Employment

Jeff Chu

EmploymentPlan.net

Copyright © 2023 by Jeff Chu

All rights reserved. No part of this book may be used or reproduced in any form whatsoever without written permission, except in the case of brief quotations in critical articles or reviews.

Published by Ekliptic,
an imprint of Sybernetics International LLC, Virginia.

Printed in the United States of America.

For more information or to book an event, contact:
jeffchu@employmentplan.net
http://www.employmentplan.net

Cover design by Ether Ling — EtherLing.com / TheCreativ.Shop
Portrait Photo by Emily Kalbaugh Photography / www.emkphoto.com

ISBN - Paperback: 978-1-952689-07-9
ISBN - eBook: 978-1-952689-02-4
Library of Congress Control Number: 2023923536

First Edition: December 2023

For Zachary

CONTENTS

Introduction 1
RESUME WRITING 5
Chapter 1: Where to Begin? 6
    Your Limited Edition 6
    What is the Purpose? 8
    One Step at a Time 11
    Planning 13
Chapter 2: How Resumes Are Read 19
    Manual Filters 19
    Automated Filters 23
    Six Second Rule 25
Chapter 3: Resume Sections 31
    A Strong Foundation 31
    Education 40
    Projects, Not Courses 44
    Experience 48
    Skills and Certifications 54
Chapter 4: The Writing Process 59
    Gather Information 59
    Action Words 65
    Placement and Order of Importance 77
    Quantify, Quantify, Quantify! 82
    Format and Readability 88
Chapter 5: Strengthening Your Resume 92
    Jargon, Space Fillers, and Generics 92
    Grammar, Spelling, and Mechanics 103
    Pitfalls and Common Mistakes 106

Chapter 6: Resume Extras 112
Career Fairs 112
Cover Letters 119
Resume Q&A 127

INTERVIEWING 131

Chapter 7: Preparing for Interviews 132
Perspective 135
Confidence 139
Avoiding Bias 146
Honesty and Integrity 150
Best Effort 152
Don't Waste Time 154

Chapter 8: Approaching Interviews 157
Prepare 157
Interview Types 168
One-on-One Interviews 169
Panel Interviews 172
Virtual Interviews 173
Phone Interviews 180
Group Interviews 183

Chapter 9: Presenting Yourself 186
Focused 186
Clear 190
Motivated 192

Chapter 10: Strategies for Questions 195
Answering Questions 195
The Power of Three 198

PAR: Problem Action Resolution..................201
Sample Interview Questions......................204
Chapter 11: Answering and Asking Questions 214
Occupation Specific Questions 214
Logic Questions.................................220
Trap Questions 224
Illegal Questions................................ 229
Interviewing for Internal Positions............................ 233
Sample Questions 237
Asking Questions 240
Questions to Ask During Internal Interviews..........244
Chapter 12: Post Interview Actions...................247
After the Interview 247
Offers and Negotiations 252
EMPLOYMENT 259
Chapter 13: The Path to a Career......................261
Your Career................................. 261
Avoid Bad Habits............................. 266
Mentoring....................................272
Networking 274
Referrals 277
Work Journals.................................279
Concluding Remarks............................. 281
Acknowledgments...............................285
About the Author 287

Introduction

Alice: Would you tell me, please, which way I ought to go from here?
The Cheshire Cat: That depends a good deal on where you want to get to.
Alice: I don't much care where.
The Cheshire Cat: Then it doesn't much matter which way you go.

- Lewis Carroll's Alice in Wonderland

Many job seekers are uncertain of what path to take for their next job or even a career. Similar to Alice, they do not know where they want to go. After finally deciding what they want to do, the task of obtaining it is daunting. Well, anything worth achieving requires a plan, and securing employment is no different. A good plan includes steps that lead toward a goal and can make achieving a seemingly impossible goal attainable.

During my senior year in high school, I thought long and hard about my future. As I pondered over what I wanted to do in life, two major goals kept entering my mind: (1)

finding long-term employment I would enjoy doing as a career, and (2) being able to make enough money to become financially independent. Well, that was a start. However, I realized that in order to achieve these goals, I would need to come up with a solid plan to go from being an applicant to being hired in a position I would find fulfilling.

After taking some time to reflect on my current academic experience, I concluded that I was a good student and was interested in law. I figured becoming a lawyer was a practical career path. It seemed that a career in law would allow me to reach my two goals of finding something I would enjoy doing and achieving financial independence.

But the requirements to become a lawyer required some major steps, such as completing an undergrad degree, taking and scoring well on the LSATS, applying to law schools, graduating law school, and passing the bar exam. I also discovered that if I failed to become a lawyer, the number of jobs I found appealing within pre-law majors alone was small. To me, this was a potential roadblock of my goals.

I decided to have a back-up plan in case I didn't become a lawyer. Since my goals could be obtained without becoming a lawyer, I concluded that I needed to pursue an undergraduate degree that would offer a more diverse career path. I found an alternative through my love for technology. The idea that technical skills could translate well in numerous employment opportunities, led me to pursue a degree in Information Systems. Fast forward a few years, and I

Introduction

discovered a passion for the technology field had surpassed my desire to become a lawyer.

This story is not to discourage readers who have a desire to pursue a career in law, but rather to explain the importance of planning. There is no wrong educational path, as long as the path you choose helps you acquire the knowledge and skills needed for your desired career.

However, you must consider other options as a means to adapt to circumstances that are possibly out of your control. To ensure the greatest possibility of success, try to have more than one path to obtaining your goals. It is through creating an effective plan that you can find clarity and practical ways forward to reach your goal.

Throughout the application process, I spent time learning from teachers, employers, and mentors. I found that for a career, I needed to work on three key areas:

1. Resume Writing
2. Interviewing
3. Employment

A solid resume is what attracts the attention of a recruiter. Strong interviewing skills instill confidence in the employer's decision to hire you. Adopting and applying exemplary habits during employment can lead you to your next position and a fulfilling career.

The purpose of this book is to equip you with the knowledge and understanding necessary to become a competitive applicant, improving your chances of being hired. To facilitate the learning process, stories and examples are used to unlock the secrets of resume writing, interviews, and employment from both the applicant's and recruiter's perspectives. Following the principles and strategies in this book will empower you on your way to crafting solid resumes, preparing for interviews, and developing desired employment qualities for a rewarding career.

RESUME WRITING

Chapter 1: Where to Begin?

Your Limited Edition

During my childhood, I developed a love for reading superhero comics. I admired the artwork and captivating storylines. I also learned that not all comics were created equal. Some of these issues were considered "limited editions." These limited editions usually had a specialized cover to signify the issue's importance. Limited edition covers were typically unique, sometimes containing better artwork, holograms, or even foil embedded into the design. Such eye-catching covers signified the rarity of the comic and indicated that the contents contained a specialized storyline. Without even seeing the words "limited edition," you could tell the issue was special just by seeing the cover alone.

A resume can be your first opportunity to catch the attention of a potential employer. It might be the first impression they have of your claimed capabilities. The goal of a resume is to stand out as a "limited edition," ultimately landing you an interview opportunity with the company.

However, if your resume is dull, hard to follow, difficult to read, or messy, your chances of getting an interview are dramatically lowered. To improve your chances, the resume sections in this book will cover many common pitfalls and misconceptions about writing a resume. After these common issues are fixed, you can focus on making your resume a "limited edition," something that reflects the quality applicant it represents.

What is the Purpose?

I was once part of a group tasked with reviewing the websites for several different departments of a company. During a business meeting, I was handed a four-page-long agenda for a meeting that was anticipated to last two hours. Now, I don't mind meetings if they are productive, but it was soon apparent this was not the case. Attendees were voicing their opinions on what should change, using drawn-out explanations to support their positions. Worst of all, no one agreed to anything.

I started to get a headache as we were getting nowhere fast, and the discussions evolved into arguments. I realized that this would continue for the entire two hours if nothing changed. At the time I was a junior-level developer and new to the company, and wondered if they would even take my thoughts into consideration.

I decided to speak up. I began by asking two simple questions: "Who exactly are the users of these sites, and what are their requirements regarding the site?" To my surprise, no one really knew the answers to the two questions I proposed. I then suggested that we postpone the rest of the meeting and focus our efforts on one site at a time, figuring out the real requirements that the users were looking for. Everyone at that moment realized the merit of my suggestion and, within five quick minutes, unanimously chose a single site to work on and reconvene on a later date. In the end, we were able to revamp the rest of the department websites through shorter meetings that had a single departmental focus.

As you prepare to write or revise a resume, you must have a purpose. Yes, it is already understood that you are applying for a position. But what position exactly are you applying for? Do you understand what the company is actually looking for? Do you comprehend what skills are required for the position?

When applying for any job, make sure that your resume actually fits the job description. If you don't have a focus, you run the risk of writing a generic resume that doesn't highlight specific experiences, skills, or knowledge of the desired qualifications.

Resume vs Curriculum Vitae (CV)
Most likely, you've heard both the terms "resume" and "CV." What is the difference between a resume and a CV? The main difference is the purpose. Resumes are used for most jobs that are more interested in your experience and skills that align with the position. For those looking at careers in the academic, medical, teaching, or research-focused positions, you are more likely to use a CV.

A resume includes only relevant items and can include:
- Education
- Experience
- Skills
- Projects or other qualifications

A CV usually includes your entire academic and research history and can include:
- Education
- Research
- Publications
- Teaching experience
- Awards, achievements, and scholarly recognitions

Another major difference between a resume and a CV is the length. Resumes are usually one to two pages in length, with a heavy focus on the first page (more on this later). A CV can be much longer than a resume due to the sheer volume of content it can contain. For the purposes of this book, the focus will be on how to write a resume. However, some of the ideas, concepts, and mechanics can be applied to both.

One Step at a Time

Improperly prioritizing a project is a personal weakness of mine. I find it difficult to see which pieces of a project are the most important parts to work on first, and I waste a lot of time trying to work on "everything" all at once. Essentially, I find that I waste a lot of time when I don't have the proper plan to start and finish a project or assignment. I'm still learning patience and working on how to pace myself accordingly While it's a lifelong process, I realized the need to address this weakness early on during my years of helping people with their resumes.

When I started offering resume writing help, I would point out all the issues and necessary changes in an individual's resume. Basically, I took the same approach I received during a high school English class – marking up the entire resume as if it were an English paper for a grade. As one of my teachers put it, there was "blood" everywhere due to all the red ink marking the mistakes. Since a resume has many different parts, marking it up the same way an English teacher would a paper might not be helpful and could become, quite honestly, overwhelming.

A recent college graduate, whom I'll call Katie, asked me to help her with her resume. Katie had been unemployed for some time and didn't know where to begin. After looking over her resume, I went to work as I usually do and made all sorts of tracked changes and comments all over her resume. When I sent it back, I told her to send me a new draft when she was done, and we could polish it up from there.

After a week passed, I decided to follow up on Katie's progress. It turns out she never finished another revision. Disappointed that my hard work seemed to go to waste, I asked her what happened. She explained that she wanted to send back a "perfect draft" with everything corrected. I realized I gave her too much to work on all at once. Katie was overwhelmed with all the suggested changes.

To help her focus, I sent her a different set of corrections that focused only on formatting. Narrowing her focus allowed her to complete the changes and send me back a revised draft. I then continued by giving her more edits, but only regarding a specific section or topic. Even though the process took a little longer, Katie successfully revised her resume.

If you're just starting a resume or trying to make revisions, it may be tempting to work on multiple aspects at once. However, the most effective way to perfect your resume is to work on one part at a time.

Planning

As a recruiter, I look at hundreds of resumes a day. The one recurring mistake I see in resumes that fail to catch my interest is that the content of the resume has very little to do with the position applied for. The largest section of these resumes often consists of previous work experiences that are not relevant to the position. There could be a number of reasons why this occurs. The most common reason is that the resume was not tailored to the position.

Your resume must have a purpose; otherwise, there's no point in creating one. It is no coincidence that the first step in resume writing is coming up with a plan. Why is a plan needed? A plan enables you to focus on obtaining the right education, training, experience, and skills that are required for a specific job or career path. Take an introspective look and identify skills or experiences you may already have that align with the position you intend to apply for.

Some applicants apply for the job simply because of the company's reputation, or they hand in their resume to me, asking me to advise them on where they could potentially fit in. From the recruiter's perspective, it shows that the applicant has not done proper research on the position or the company itself.

Remember, the only one responsible for your career path is none other than yourself. Take time to research positions and companies that genuinely interest you. Then, evaluate the experience, skills, knowledge, and abilities you currently have that qualify you for the position. Should you find gaps in any of the areas, start working on obtaining these qualifications before you even apply for the position.

Rather than asking the recruiter where you belong, tell the recruiter what position you qualify for and why you should be hired. You don't want someone else in charge of your career. The most successful applicants, and ultimately those who become some of the best employees, are those who have a clear understanding of their career goals and are confident about the positions they aim to be hired for. This kind of confidence also helps the recruiter in their decision-making process when moving applicants forward.

There are so many instances where I have heard applicants say, "I just want to get my foot in the door." When I hear this, I may ask:

- Why do you want to work for us?
- What position do you really want?
- What experience and skills do you have that qualify you for the position?
- How satisfied are you going to be working in the position you are interviewing for?
- What happens if you are unable to move to the position you want?

These are just some questions to get you thinking. If you're just starting out, look at the opportunities you are interested in and read the job descriptions. To make things easier on yourself, pick several jobs that have similar responsibilities and qualifications. This way, you are not narrowing your search too much. Once you've identified several positions you wish to pursue, assess whether there are any qualifications you lack.

Let's take a look at an example job posting:

Entry Data Scientist Position

Qualifications
- Bachelor's degree or Master's degree in Computer Engineering, Computer Science, or Mathematics.
- Must have Mathematics or Statistics background.
- Experience in Python programming and understanding of the software development life cycle.
- Excellent written and verbal communication skills.
- Able to perform data analysis and visualization
- Highly motivated, self-learner, team player, and technically inquisitive.
- Strong work ethics and creative problem-solving abilities.

Responsibilities
- Assess project requirements and develop data analysis algorithms.
- Collaborate with developers, sharing opinions, knowledge, and recommendations.
- Provide technical solutions, conduct software analyses, ability to interpret big data sets, and create visualizations.
- Integrate components like UI web applications, commercial indexing products, and access control.

Take note of two separate qualifications.

1. Hard skills: Skills that are defined as occupation specific. These skills are often quantifiable or measurable and can be acquired through education and training. In the context of this example, the following are hard skills:

- Bachelor's degree or Master's degree in Computer Engineering, Computer Science, or Mathematics.
- Must have Mathematics or Statistics background.
- Experience in Python programming and understanding of the software development life cycle.
- Able to perform data analysis and visualization

2. Soft skills: Attributes or personality traits that generally pertain to interpersonal interactions. These skills are commonly acquired through feedback from our experiences in various situations.

- Highly motivated, self-learner, team player, and technically inquisitive.
- Excellent written and verbal communication skills.
- Strong work ethics and creative problem-solving abilities.

This is just one example of a job position. When you're in the process of exploring potential job opportunities, take time to examine several positions that capture your interest. Identify common qualifications that attract you, and then see which qualifications overlap. Start looking into positions that overlap in skills and experience.

One exercise you can attempt involves creating Venn Diagrams, which can assist you in visualizing the overlaps in terms of educational background, training, skills, and experience required for various positions. For example, if there are several positions you are considering that require the same educational degree, it might be worthwhile to pursue that specific educational requirement.

To help visualize this concept, below is an example using our previously mentioned Entry Data Scientist position and then comparing it to a sample Entry Python Developer position. While there are differences in the requirements for each position, there are also overlaps. Starting with the qualifications that overlap can help broaden the positions you can apply for.

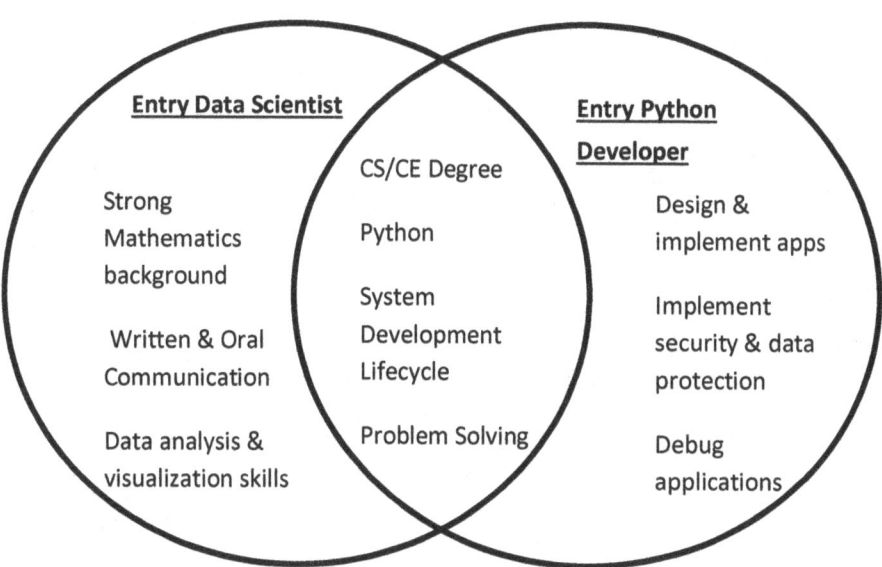

In this Venn Diagram example, the overlap–or the middle area—represents the primary qualification that should be the initial focus. By working on building up education and experience in the middle area, the individual will already start developing their resume for a broader number of positions. You never want to narrow your focus to a niche market, or you may find yourself in a difficult position when searching for what you want to do. Remember, always have a contingency plan.

Chapter 2: How Resumes Are Read

Manual Filters

The goal of a resume is to secure yourself an interview. However, before employers begin interviewing, all resumes are filtered either manually, electronically, or both. Recruiters often look for specific items on a resume before delving deeper. Companies typically have a checklist of essential skills or experiences to "screen out" or "filter" resumes. As previously mentioned, a job posting will have some required or desired qualifications. While the ideal applicant would possess all of these, in reality, some qualifications may carry more weight than others.

For instance, if a company requires a bachelor's degree in finance or a similar field, the recruiter might look for this requirement specifically and immediately decide to place your resume in the "no" pile if you have anything other than that. This is a rather stringent example, but recruiters use this in order to save time, especially when dealing with a large stack of resumes.

One time as a recruiter I was trying to fill five entry-level business analyst positions. The positions were all the same and required two specific skills: Tableau and SQL. I had a stack of over 200 resumes, and in order to get through the pile to find my five applicants, I went looking only for these two hard skills. If any resume did not have both skills, it went in the "no" pile.

By the end, I had a stack of 50 resumes with the required two skills. Based on this one filter, I eliminated 150 resumes. Did I throw away great applicants based on this filter? Certainly. However, as a recruiter, you don't have the luxury of asking each applicant if they accidentally left off the required skills.

My next hard requirement was experience in either data analytics, data science, or business analytics. With the 50 resumes I had left, I looked at each resume's job experience section and looked for those specific positions. To account for some variability, I did consider job titles that could be relatable to the position I was looking for.

After this scrutiny, only 20 resumes remained. A more in-depth examination of these 20 left me with 10 that closely aligned with my criteria. I then ranked them and started the process of contacting each applicant to conduct interviews.

I hope this experience provides you some clarity on a possible scenario that your resume will go through. There will always be certain objectives a recruiter will look for on your resume. You'll want to ensure that these items can be found quickly and easily.

It's not practical for a recruiter to read every word on a resume. As a recruiter, I try to create an objective way to consistently look at each resume. For each position, I create an outline of the essential skills, experience, and credentials required. This helps me hone my focus to find what I am looking for.

At a Glance
Formatting/Look and Feel
- How is the look and feel of the resume?
- Is the resume difficult to read, and are things hard to find?
- Are there any inconsistencies, missing information, grammar mistakes, or typos?

Experience and Skills
- Does it contain the key skills (must haves) for the position?
- Do the job titles make sense, and are they applicable to the position?

Longer Looks
Relevant Work Experience
- Does it contain relevant soft and hard skills?
- Does it contain jargon, space fillers, or generic lines?
- Does the resume just list keywords, or does it showcase the experience level or application of the skills.
- Do the descriptions merely state job roles, or do they detail specific accomplishments?
- What is the level of experience?
- How many years of relevant work experience?
- Are there big breaks in the timeline?
- Are relevant certifications up-to-date?
- Does the resume show a history of jumping from employer to employer or consistency in staying with companies?
- When will they graduate, or how long has it been since the applicant has been out of school?

Every recruiter is either taught a certain way to filter applicants from their company or develops an individual list of what is considered important for the position. Some lists will contain bias, but having a set standard is a way for the company to filter through resumes in a consistent manner.

Automated Filters

To save time, some companies invest in automating the initial resume screening process using Applicant Tracking System (ATS). This software assists companies in streamlining the hiring process. Often it can scan and score a resume according to how closely the content fits a set of parameters or job requirements. If the resume has a high score or meets the threshold set by the company, then and only then it moves forward in the application process. Eventually, the resume is looked at by an actual human being.

It's important to carefully read the required and desired qualifications for any position. Look for keywords and add all of the ones you have. If you are missing any, start working on those skills or qualifications until you can add them to your resume. Chances are, a similar job position in the future will have that requirement as well.

Remember, even if your resume passes an ATS, a person will still review it. Because of this, you don't want to merely stuff your resume with a listing of keywords. Try to create a balance between keywords and detailing your experience level in those skills, or how you have applied them.

- **Use a file format the ATS can read:** Ensure your resume can be read by the ATS software the company uses. A digital resume is usually in PDF format. Some ATS software may not be able to read the resume properly if it expects a particular format. For any application, find out what file format is acceptable.

- **Stick to standard fonts:** To avoid readability issues, stick to conventional fonts that any ATS can recognize such as Calibri, Cambria, Georgia, or Times New Roman...etc. Another test is to use a font that isn't distracting when read by a real person.

- **Prioritize text over graphics:** Avoid items that ATS may have trouble reading. Your resume should primarily be text in order to facilitate the readability of your resume to an ATS. Regardless of whether your resume is reviewed by an ATS or not, the following list are items you should remove as they can seem out of place or distracting to the reader:

    - Charts
    - Shapes
    - Colors
    - Graphs
    - Graphics
    - Images/Pictures
    - Unique characters

Six Second Rule

Let's play a quick game!

To play, you will need the following:

- Something or someone to time you.
- Something to write on and write with.

The following are the rules and instructions:

On the next page, you will see a series of words. Take a look at the list of words for six seconds.

- After six seconds, close the book.
- Finally, see how many you can recall.
- Do not cheat!

Ready? Go!

Foods February Turtle Pizza Blue January Bird Burgers Red Colors March Dog Ice Cream Yellow Pets May Cake Cat Green Months

How did you do? How many did you recall?

Let's try this one more time.

Do not use the previous page; instead, use the next page, following the same rules as before. Ready? Go!

Months	Foods	Pets	Colors
• January	• Burgers	• Bird	• Blue
• February	• Cake	• Cat	• Green
• March	• Ice	• Dog	• Red
• April	Cream	• Turtle	• Yellow

How did you do the second time? You should have done much better! I hope you had fun playing this little game. What was the point, you ask? Well, this leads into the important litmus test of a resume. The six second rule. Throughout my experiences with reviewing resumes, all too often I have seen individuals who usually fall into one of two categories:

1) Those who write too little.
2) Those who write too much.

How does one know what constitutes as too little and how much is too much? What is the right balance? The key is a strong basic structure. A clear, easy to read, structured resume will enhance your chances of passing the initial screening.

Imagine manning your company's booth to chat with potential recruits for several hours. In addition, you spend time scanning hundreds of resumes, conducting interviews, and shortlisting the ones to proceed further in the hiring process. That's how a recruiter's time can be spent during a career fair! But to get to the interview stage, an applicant's resume must first clear the scan. While it's wishful thinking that a recruiter will read every word on your resume, that's rarely the reality.

Many companies, especially large ones, will receive hundreds of resumes each day. This leads into what I call the *'six second resume rule'*. Someone other than you should be able to pick up your resume and glean enough information in six seconds to understand what kind of experience you have had and your educational background. However, in roughly six seconds, it should also be apparent what kind of skills you have associated with those experiences. You can test this by giving your resume to a trusted friend and timing them. If, within the first six seconds, your friend is struggling to find information, it's time to restructure.

Chapter 3: Resume Sections

A Strong Foundation

A resume must have a logical flow. Even if you have the most amazing experience and skills for the position, if the recruiter struggles to find or understand them in your resume, then none of it matters. To simplify this approach, focus on creating an organized structure where anyone reading your resume can quickly find what they are looking for.

A typical resume should not be longer than a page, especially if you're still in school or at the beginning of your career. Only after you have acquired a larger track record of relevant experience and are in the middle of your career or applying for a position that requires significant experience and abilities should you go over a page. If you decide to go over a page, your first page must have enough information to capture the reader's attention.

For starters, a basic resume should have a few key sections, like the following:

- Header
- Education
- Experience
- Projects
- Skills

Header

Education

Experience

Projects

Skills

Except for the header, you can rearrange other sections where it makes the most sense. For example, if you completed your education and have been in the workforce for a few years, education should be at the end. The focus near the top should be on relevant work experience.

Header

The header should be the first part of your resume. It should contain your name and contact information in a manner that does not take up an exorbitant amount of space. All information should be clear and easy to read.

Contact Information

There's no point in having a great resume if the recruiter is unable to contact you. At the very least, make sure in your resume you have listed at least two valid ways to reach you. Try not to limit the ways a recruiter can reach out to you. The minimum should be a phone number and an email address.

Phone Number

Include only one phone number where you can be reached. If you list a phone number, make sure it's a number that works. Employers and recruiters will prefer different means of communication. Some prefer to contact applicants through text or email, while others may use landlines to call. Silencing unknown callers may prevent you from being reached, as unknown calls are sometimes sent directly to voicemail. If your voice box is full, it will make it even more difficult for the employer to reach you.

When returning a phone call to an employer or recruiter, sometimes you may have to leave a message if you are calling after hours. Make sure you leave your name and number. I have had numerous messages from potential applicants who never left a call-back number or just their first name. Do not assume they will recognize your voice or have time to check call logs. Making it easy for the recruiter to get back to you is key. You are not the only applicant the recruiter is trying to get a hold of.

Email

To reduce bias, try to have an email address that is professional. An unprofessional email address could portray negative implications. Stay away from using emails that are immature, sexual in nature, or have profanity/slang. If you create a new email for your job searches, make sure it's an account you will regularly check.

Make sure your email address is simple. Your name or a variation of it should be the logical choice. If your email address is too long, contains a lot of numbers/characters, or is easily mistyped, then there is a chance a recruiter will send an email to the wrong address.

Physical Address – Optional

Clients of mine have asked if a mailing address is important. With other forms of communication, such as texting and email, an address may not seem necessary. The answer honestly depends on the company you are applying for.

- **Expected/Required** – In a historical sense, including an address has been standard practice. An employer may expect to see this information on your resume. At some point in the application process, you will eventually need to provide a real address.

    Another small benefit of listing an address is that it helps the recruiter. An address allows the recruiter to call at an appropriate time. For example, if the employer resides on the east coast and it's 8 AM, it will be 5 AM on the West Coast. If the recruiter is aware their applicant is on the West Coast, they will most likely try to call at a later time.

- **ATS Records** – Some employers require an address as part of their application process. If they use an ATS, your resume will be scanned, and an address helps with pre-populating an applicant record. The more information you have, the more complete your record will be, and the easier it is to find your information when they need it.

- **Relocation** – If you are not local to the company's location, a recruiter may favor an applicant who is more local. This could be due to avoiding relocation costs or a greater probability that the applicant will stay long term due to already living in the area. If the position does not have telecommuting or remote work, the company will want to ensure you are okay with relocating.

If you are not local, make sure you and anyone that will move with you are okay with relocation if the company requires you to work in the area. It's a waste of time, regardless of how qualified you are, if you are unwilling to move for a position that requires you to be there in person. As a recruiter, I have wasted a lot of time on applicants who did not speak with their significant other, spouse, or dependents prior to applying for a position that required relocation.

- **Personally Identifiable Information (PII)** – While recruiters should be trained on how to properly handle PII, there is always a chance your resume has too much PII that can be misused/mishandled. If you are worried about your PII being misused should your resume fall into the wrong hands, you can write just the city and state on the resume, then provide your full address at a later point, such as an official application, when it's required. This might be equally true if you are using a third-party recruiting site that is directly affiliated with the company you want to apply for.

Let's look at an example of a header:

> # Jane R. Smith
> ## Orem, UT | (801) 100-0000 | j.smith@email.com
> ---

In this example, there is almost no differentiation in format, making it harder to distinguish the most important piece of information, your name. Also, while the contact information is there, it takes up two lines. Let's try to format it a bit.

Jane R. Smith

Orem, UT | (801) 100-0000 | j.smith@email.com | https://git.io/ZfzQl
---

This revised header reduces the information to two lines. The name is bold and larger in size than other parts of the header. This allows it to stand out more than the contact information. Since we read from left to right, aligning the text to the left allows the reader to also begin at the left rather than the center of the page. By aligning left, there is actually more space, which allows for the addition of a work sample link.

External Links

One thing you can add is a profile link (such as LinkedIn), a personal website, or some other means to showcase work samples, projects, or other information. For individuals who can code, there is GitHub. There are other social media platforms that can serve as a portfolio for your work as well.

While not all recruiters will take the time to look at these links, they can serve as another means to widen your job search net or be discovered by a recruiter. These links should be consistent with and compliment your resume. They should also provide supplemental information that enhances or goes beyond what is in your resume.

Remember, the reviewer of your resume will only go to these if they have the time and if they feel your resume already has something they are interested in. In other words, if your resume isn't interesting, they will not take the time to go to these supplemental links. When deciding to add links to your resume, ask yourself the following questions:

- **Is all the content up-to-date?** I once received a resume with a link to the individual's LinkedIn profile. When I viewed the profile, it was apparent the profile had not been updated for quite some time, and the status even listed the individual as on sabbatical.

- **Does it display your best work?** If a recruiter takes the time to visit a link you listed, make sure it adds value. The point is to showcase more of what you can do. If it's not impressive, it could backfire. One student's resume listed a GitHub link that contained only one unfinished school assignment.

- **Is it accessible?** Make sure the link is correct and actually works. This may seem obvious, but I have found resumes with links that were either not active or were incorrect, and I was unable to view the site or profile. Another issue could be assuming I already have an account on that platform. If you're using a very unique platform, does it require a user to register to view the content, or can anyone with the link access it?

Education

Recent Graduate Resumes
Your education should be the first section and should at least include the college you are attending, your major, the projected month and year of graduation, and your current GPA. If you have multiple degrees, start with the highest and then list the others, each time providing the same details. However, if you have three or more degrees, you should have only degrees related to the position listed.

As a recruiter, the major and degree are often more significant than the institution attended. Similar to how I valued the title of the position over the name of the company in the experience section.

Working Professional
As mentioned earlier, if you have completed your education and have relevant work experience, your education section should be at the end of your resume. The most important part of your educational history would be your degree and major. Your major should be in a relevant field for the position you are applying for.

Education should take up as little space as possible. If

you can, try to fit this information into two lines on your resume per relevant degree. This should display your major and degree, the name of the institution, and the year you graduated. You should only list your highest degree unless your lesser degrees are relevant. If you have two advanced degrees, the most relevant to the job is the one you place first.

Education

Master of Science Data Science — May 20XX
University of California, Los Angeles – GPA 3.97

Bachelor of Science Computer Science — May 20XX
University of California, Los Angeles – GPA 3.88

Minimum GPA

Grades are only one data point in the review process, but they are an important one for applicants still working on their educational pursuits. Even though grades do not determine success in the workforce, they might be one of the factors an employer considers if the applicant is a student.

A Grade Point Average (GPA) is an easy standard an employer can set to filter applicants quickly. If you are currently a student applying for an internship or a job, one of your goals is to obtain a GPA that is higher than what is listed in the qualifications of the position. Your major should also be in a field that is relevant to the position you are applying for.

There are two types of GPAs you can list on your

resume. The first is cumulative. This is the GPA that accounts for all courses you have taken, including generals and extracurriculars. The second is your major GPA. This is the GPA of just your major's relevant coursework. This gives you two chances to make the minimum target GPA to be a competitive applicant. However, make a note if it is the major GPA in your resume that you are listing.

If the position requires a GPA of 3.0, go beyond the minimum. A safe target would be to maintain at least a 3.5 GPA or higher in order to stand out a bit more than other applicants. However, if your GPA is lower than a 3.0, understand that you will not be competitive in comparison to other applicants. Because of this, you're going to need to have stronger qualifications either in terms of relevant work experience or some other unique factor, to give you more of a competitive edge.

With a GPA below a 3.0, you can leave it off your resume, but it will raise questions as to why it was not listed. You can still apply for the position if the GPA is the only piece you lack, but just know that recruiters may see that as a red flag and may not even look at your resume if you don't meet this minimum qualification.

For applicants who have been out of school for quite some time, you can leave off your GPA, as your relevant experience should be the focus.

Optional: Awards and Achievements
Scholarships and academic achievements such as Dean's Lists

or other noteworthy accomplishments can be good to have on a resume. It can show that you were able to reach a higher level of excellence than your peers. If you list them, make sure the achievement can be understood by anyone reading your resume.

Projects, Not Courses

If you have a lot of work experience relevant to the position you are applying for, then you do not need this section. However, if you are indeed struggling to even fill out a one-page resume, you can put in course work that relates to the job you are applying for. If you choose to do this section, leave course numbers and course names out.

For example, a recruiter will not know what ACC221 is. Similarly, while a recruiter may have an idea of what Advanced Accounting Principles are, they won't know exactly what is taught. The course title is often not descriptive enough. You want to highlight relevant projects you have done for the class. Basically, you can write them in a way that mirrors the work experience section. The next page contains an example of how this can be portrayed.

Academic Writing and Presentations

The Economic Impacts of the US and China Trade War   **Mar 20XX**
- Wrote a comprehensive research paper that overviews US and China relations, the impact of US tariffs on China, and an outlook of the effects of the trade war on the US economy.
- Researched academic journals and conducted statistical analysis of economic data.
- Published in Vol. 2, Issue 12 (2022) of the Asian Studies Student Association Academic Journal.

Presentation on Hong Kong Democracy Protests   **Dec 20XX**
- Briefed a 20-minute presentation to a class of 25 students on the impact of China's National Security Laws, the current state of protests in Hong Kong, and the impact on Hong Kong's democracy.

This fictitious example displays a few things.

- **Skills/Abilities:** Samples of the applicant's experience of writing, researching, and briefing. These may be key qualifications required for the job.

- **Knowledge:** The topics in the research paper and presentation show the applicant may have research and academic knowledge of certain topics. In this example, China, Hong Kong, and economy.

- **Scale:** Quantification helps the recruiter see size of

audience the individual has briefed.

Another step to make this even better would be a link to the paper or slides of the presentation. This would allow the recruiter to view the work and determine the actual quality if you aren't able to include the writing sample in your application. Remember, recruiters do not care what you learned, but rather how you have applied it and the impact.

Let's take a look at another example for a technical position:

Personal Technical Projects

Asian Fusion Cuisine Website   **Dec 20XX**
- Designed a website with HTML, JavaScript, CSS for a restaurant start-up and crafted an interactive Asian fusion menu. – www.asiafusion2go.com

COVID0-19 Forecast and Dashboard   **Jun 20XX - Aug 20XX**
- Analyzed vaccination data vs infection rates, built 10 data visuals, and predicted future trends using Python, SQL, and Tableau.
- Presented to five local community leaders in a virtual setting to push awareness of findings, resulting in the organization of three vaccination clinics.

- **Technical skills**: The first project, rather than just having a listing of technical languages, displays how the individual used HTML, JavaScript, CSS in a website, and gives a link to the website. The second explains how Python, SQL, and Tableau were used to analyze and forecast COVID-19 infection rates, and created data visuals.

- **Soft skills**: Presentation, communication, leadership, and organizational skills are highlighted in the second project. There is even an impact of the project with the local community. Even though there is no link to the project, if this individual received an interview, the interviewer could ask to see the project to gain a better picture of the individual's skill level.

Projects like these demonstrate initiative, thoughtfulness, and hands-on experience. When guiding applicants with limited experience, I emphasize that, while nothing can truly replace relevant work experience, a personal project can occasionally be a more telling indicator of one's capabilities than an assigned academic project. This is especially true if it showcases the skills demanded by the job in question. Learn to learn independently, and learn to build your skills toward the career you want.

Experience

Throughout college, I pursued a degree in Information Systems. During that time, I looked for technical jobs, as that was my career path. There was just one problem: I had little to no technical experience. As I tried to write my resume, I found that I didn't have enough experience to even fill up an entire page.

I then decided to get help from my business writing professor. I explained to him that I was having trouble writing my resume since I had so little experience to show. The professor smiled, and then asked me a simple question: "How old are you?" I replied, "I'm 21." He then wisely replied, "Then you have 21 years of experience. As a young man at your age, there should be plenty of experiences you can draw from. You just need to think about what they are."

Your experience section is perhaps the most essential part of your resume, as it should explain what you have done that relates to the position. The stronger this section is, the better chance you have of getting an interview.

One of the most common problems a person faces when writing a resume is having relevant work experience. However, everything you do in life can count as experience. While not in all cases, in many instances, experience from a job in one area can translate into another.

Relevant Work Experience

Relevant work experience should and will always supersede anything you may lack in education. While it does not replace an educational requirement, a good recruiter will recognize and value someone with proven experience over someone with only academic knowledge of how to work in the field.

Granted, formal education in the field is crucial — and sometimes essential for job security or to avoid hitting a career ceiling — but relevant work experience can often be more instrumental in securing a job. The best, of course, is to have both education and relevant experience.

Volunteer Experience

Experience does not always need to be from a job that you were paid for. Volunteer work can also translate into experience that you can and should include on your resume. If you volunteer at church, clubs, or organizations, consider how these experiences relate to the position you're applying for.

For example, if you served in a leadership position, participated in collaborative projects, or used a skill relevant to the positions you are applying for, these can and should count as experience.

Let's take a look at an example of how we can display volunteer experience on a resume.

Volunteer Experience

Student Editor — Dec 20XX – Present
Self-employed – Remote
- Edited over 60 student research papers and provided feedback on proper APA, MLA, and Chicago Manual of Style formats.

Translator – Mandarin Chinese — Jul 20XX – Jan 20XX
Community Church – Brooklyn, NY
- Translated verbal weekly church services to Mandarin speaking congregation of 40 members.
- Assisted community leaders in translation of written materials for Chinese Community.

Vice President — May 20XX – Sep 20XX
Asian Student Union – Brooklyn, NY
- Collaborated and helped organize monthly events for Asian student community.
- Led a team of 20 students to create a Lunar New Year event for over 100 attendees – efforts included organizing speakers, food, activities, and advertising for the event.

This shows an individual with some experience using skills that a job posting might be looking for.

- Experience in editing and using standard writing formats, such as APA, MLA, and Chicago Manual Style.

- Mandarin Chinese language skills in both reading and speaking.

- Ability to lead a group and work collaboratively with others.

Find Relevant Experience

One summer, during my sophomore year in college, I worked as a student counselor. My educational track was actually in Information Systems, and I knew I really needed to start getting job experience in more technical fields of study. Because of this, I volunteered to be the technical support for the counselors and assisted them with all tech-related issues.

The program itself was well-constructed and had a fast-paced training plan to help prepare new counselors for the summer ahead. I remember on my first day, I was handed a huge binder that was full of documents explaining everything in detail. Given the tight training timeline, sifting through this binder often felt like wading through an avalanche of information.

The hardest part was leafing through the binder to locate specific documentation for particular activities. When our time as counselors concluded, we were tasked with documenting our experiences and learnings to help future counselors prepare and improve upon our experience.

I decided that there was not only a better way to improve the training part of the program, but also for the guide to be more accessible (and, of course, to save trees). After I pitched my idea to the director of the summer program about creating a digital guide, he was very interested. But explained that there would be no such funding available to create the digital guide. I then told him I would do it for free as long as I could claim the experience and credit for the program. He willingly agreed, and I went to work and created a digital website version that allowed for easier navigation to specific documents and links to media files. Since the University had many ways to host digital content securely, the guide could be placed there with no issues.

I tell this story to simply highlight the fact that if I was able to change my experience as a student counselor into a technical work experience, so can you. I undertook the technical aspects of the program and then furthered my technical skills in web design when I volunteered my time to create a more efficient guide for the program.

Experience

Student Counselor   **May 20XX – Jul 20XX**
Brigham Young University – Provo, UT
- Designed and developed a new student counselor training webpage using HTML, JavaScript, and CSS for future student counselors, resulting in a digitized and accessible version of all training materials.
- Served a technical support for BYU's Multicultural Student Service's – troubleshooting technical connectivity and presentation equipment.
- Counseled and mentored over 30 high school students preparing to enter college.

In some cases, we don't get the opportunity to gain the qualifications necessary for a position. Because of this, we need to find or create our own experiences that can relate to the job requirements. If there is a particular career path you are seeking, find innovative ways to develop the skills necessary for that position. This can be done through using current skills to solve problems or looking for added responsibilities to develop them. Once achieved, these can be added to your resume.

Skills and Certifications

Jobs demanding specific skill sets or familiarity with tools, such as particular software, often have associated professional certifications or exams. If you have had any type of certified training that is sought after or required for the position, make sure that it is current and relevant to the position.

Certifications that are not directly related but contain transferrable skills may still be valuable enough to include them in your resume. Ensure these certifications are visible in their section, list the official title and any associated ID number for verification.

For clarity, always spell out acronyms unless you're confident the hiring manager will recognize them immediately (e.g., if the position lists the certification as a required qualification for the position). Using the full official names or expanding acronyms ensures that even those unfamiliar with the certification can easily look it up online. Always specify either the precise date you earned the certification or its expiration date.

If you have foreign language skills, you will need to explain the proficiency level you are at. You can accomplish this in several different ways, but be consistent with whatever you choose. You can list language exam scores, explain proficiency, or quantify your use of the language in years.

> **Foreign Language Skills**
>
> - **Mandarin Chinese** – Native Level proficiency in reading, writing, and speaking
> - **Japanese** – Limited working proficiency in speaking and reading

Proficiency

You can add words to explain the proficiency level if you are going to list skills. It's better to be upfront about the level of your skills to help the recruiter know what questions to ask you.

When I interview applicants, I try to give them a fair opportunity to prove what they actually know. For example, I will lean towards questions on skills that an applicant has more experience in rather than ones that they are currently learning or are new to. This approach helps me understand their current competencies. If I want to test them for potential, I might adjust questions on skills that they are currently learning by teaching a short concept or topic on the matter and then seeing if they can think of when to apply it.

In the Technical Skill section on the next page, I would most likely ask the individual more questions on Java, JavaScript, or SQL rather than C++, Angular, and Tableau.

Technical Skills

- Experienced: Java - 6+ years, JavaScript - 6+ years, and SQL - 4 years
- Developmental: C++, Angular, and Tableau

Up-To-Date

Recruiters want to know if your certifications are up-to-date. For any certifications, ensure that you have the dates of when you were either awarded the certification or when it expires. Make sure you are clear if you are working towards the certification that is in progress of completion, and note when you intend to certify. Do not claim a certification you don't intend on completing.

Certifications

- Certified Scrum Master (CSM) — **Certified 20XX**
- Scaled Agile Framework (SAFe) — **Certified 20XX**
- Project Management Professional (PMP) — **In Progress**
  - Certification through Project Management Institute (PMI)
  - Exam scheduled November 202X

Clearances and Professional Licenses

Some positions have a hard requirement for which there are no exceptions, such as a security clearance, required license, or certification. Have these near the top of your resume to ensure the recruiter sees this qualification at the start. Always include the date of expiration or when you were last active if it's currently inactive. If applicable, include the ID number to help the recruiter save time in verifying your credentials.

Professional Certifications

- **Active Pharmacist License:** Virginia #0000000001
- **Basic Life Support Certified:** ID# 200000 valid until August 20XX
- **American Public Health Association (APhA) Immunization Certified:** September 2, 20XX

Remove Generics and Basics

As a recruiter, I have seen numerous resumes that have a skills section that lists something like the following:

Skills

- Office Administration
- Business Analysis
- Customer Service
- Team Player
- Microsoft Word
- Microsoft PowerPoint
- Microsoft Excel

This example displays skills that are generic, are soft skills, or are basic technical skills. Such skills should be either left off or baked into your experience bullets. For example, instead of listing "team player," use a bullet point to explain how you collaborated with other coworkers. I've also observed such skills represented as a bar chart, which is not recommended. This is ineffective since the scale is usually subjective and there's no objective way to measure a soft skill (more on this later).

Microsoft Office Suite and its products are too basic to place on a resume, especially if you are applying for a technical position. It is assumed all applicants have a working knowledge of it. The exception to this is if the position directly requires skill with Microsoft Office. Then you should have it listed, but clarify your proficiency level with it. Go beyond a list. It doesn't tell the recruiter how good you are with it or what experience you've had.

Chapter 4: The Writing Process

Gather Information

On numerous occasions, I receive a resume that is missing information. Gaps such as inconsistent dates, missing locations, and incomplete employment histories are some of the basic information that, when left out, creates issues during a resume review. When a resume is missing information, the applicant loses credibility, and the reviewer does not have enough information to make a decision on whether or not to move the applicant forward in the hiring process. As a result, such resumes usually don't move forward in the application process.

In one case, a college student named Brian sought my help in improving his resume. Let's take a look:

> **Brian M.**
> Vienna, VA | 703-200-000 | brian@example.com
>
> **Education**
> **Bachelor's in Global Affairs**
> Sep 20XX – Present
>
>
> **Work Experience**
> **Harris Teeter**
> **Jan 20XX – Present**
> Cashier, Express Lane Shopper
>
> **McDonald's Crew Member**
> **McDonald's**
> **20XX – 20XX**
> Mainly Cashier, some kitchen work
>
> **Taco Bell Crew Member**
> **Taco Bell**
> **20XX – 20XX**
>
>
> **Skills**
> Fluent in Arabic, Microsoft Office, Cash handling, Communication, Customer Service

It's clear that the above resume contains numerous issues with consistency, formatting, and content. However, some of the more pressing issues with the resume is missing or incomplete information about his education and relevant experience. For starters, in the education section, basic information is missing, such as the institution's name and the GPA. Throughout the resume, dates are also inconsistent, as they bounce from month and year to just years listed.

Earlier in this book, I discussed the importance of understanding the requirements for positions you are interested in. Hopefully, by now, you have an idea of the requirements for the types of jobs you are considering, and have begun to evaluate what you've already accomplished or are working on that qualifies you for the position. If your qualifications seem limited, then start considering which qualifications you can work on now to fill in these gaps. You may need to pursue more education, complete some personal projects, or acquire relevant experiences that can enhance those qualifications.

As I continued to work with Brian on his resume, I asked him what kind of position he was applying for. He then explained that he was applying for a position as an Arabic translator. In its current state, Brian's experience section of his resume contained nothing regarding his proficiency in Arabic. Instead, it emphasized the part-time jobs he held at fast-food restaurants and grocery stores. I do want to be clear that there is nothing wrong with taking these types of jobs, since all work experience teaches you skills that are valuable for growth and provide a source of income. However, these positions unfortunately do not provide a lot of competitive experience for a position as an Arabic translator.

There are now two ways he can approach improving his resume's experience section.

- Improve his work experience section to highlight the skills that might relate to other aspects of the position's qualifications.

- Look for other experience that is more relevant to the position.

I proceeded by asking Brian if he had done any volunteer service as a translator or even used it in a work capacity. He then mentioned several volunteer positions at his church and at a local newspaper, where he used his Arabic language to help translate verbal and written communication. Now we are on to something that is directly related to the position!

The next step in improving Brian's resume was to gather all the information about his previous experiences, both volunteer and paid, that relate to the position. To keep things simple, I told him that to think of one experience at a time and that it could be out of chronological order. We just wanted to get things down on paper. For each experience, he was to only focus on all the basic information:

- **Position/Title:** If you don't have a specific title, use a title that can be understood by anyone. However, be realistic with your titles. Do not embellish.

- **Company or organization:** You can use either the official name of the employer/organization, or one that is more easily recognized if they are known by other names. For example, Virginia Tech's official name is Virginia Polytechnic Institute and State University. However, more people would recognize "Virginia Tech".

- **Location:** Having the city and state can give the recruiter an idea of where you have worked. If you are out of the country, clarify what country and city you were in.

- **Dates:** When you list the dates that you worked, make sure you are consistent throughout. Have at least the month and year.

To help organize this information, we created separate boxes with the basic information filled in for each position. It looked like the following:

- **Title:** Arabic Interpreter
- **Organization:** Fairfax County
- **Location:** Fairfax, VA
- **Dates:** Dec 20XX – Present

- **Title:** Arabic Translator
- **Organization:** Kuwait Newspaper
- **Location:** Shuwaikh Industrial, Kuwait
- **Dates:** Feb 20XX – Dec 20XX

- **Title:** Arabic Translator
- **Organization:** Christian Church
- **Location:** Vienna, VA
- **Dates:** Sep 19XX – Dec 20XX

Now that we had all the basic information, we could start brainstorming what was actually done in each of these positions.

Action Words

There are words that draw attention to experience lines in your resume. These are specific verbs or action words that highlight a specific skill or accomplishment. If used correctly, they can quickly signal to the reviewer what types of experiences you have. For example, if you are looking for a management position, your resume needs to reflect words that convey leadership, team building, or project ownership. The trick is to think of qualities the position requires, and then find action words that define those qualities.

Writing these action words down can also help you categorize your experiences. Categorizing experiences can make interview preparation easier. The next two pages contain a list of topically organized action words that can help you get started when thinking of your experiences. There are other similar lists on the internet if you're not seeing a word that defines your experience accurately.

Achievement
- Attained
- Awarded
- Completed
- Earned
- Exceeded
- Outperformed
- Reached
- Showcased
- Succeeded
- Surpassed
- Targeted

Acquisitions
- Acquired
- Forged
- Navigated
- Partnered
- Secured

Advisory
- Advised
- Advocated
- Arbitrated
- Coached
- Consulted
- Educated
- Fielded
- Informed
- Resolved

Changes/Improvements
- Centralized
- Clarified
- Converted
- Customized
- Improved
- Influenced
- Integrated
- Merged
- Modified
- Overhauled
- Redesigned
- Refocused
- Reorganized
- Replaced
- Restructured
- Revamped
- Simplified
- Streamlined
- Updated
- Upgraded
- Transformed

Increased
- Accelerated
- Achieved
- Advanced
- Amplified
- Boosted
- Capitalized
- Delivered
- Enhanced
- Expedited
- Furthered
- Gained
- Generated
- Improved
- Lifted
- Maximized
- Outpaced
- Stimulated
- Sustained

Leadership
- Chaired
- Controlled
- Coordinated
- Executed
- Headed
- Led
- Managed
- Operated
- Orchestrated
- Organized
- Oversaw
- Planned
- Produced

Management
- Aligned
- Cultivated
- Directed
- Enabled
- Facilitated
- Fostered
- Hired
- Inspired
- Mentored
- Mobilized
- Recruited
- Regulated
- Supervised
- Taught
- Trained
- Unified
- United

Action Words

Production
- Administered
- Built
- Charted
- Created
- Designed
- Developed
- Devised
- Founded
- Engineered
- Established
- Founded
- Formulated
- Implemented
- Initiated
- Instituted
- Introduced
- Launched
- Pioneered
- Provided
- Spearheaded

Saving Time or Money
- Conserved
- Consolidated
- Decreased
- Deducted
- Lessened
- Reconciled
- Reduced
- Saved
- Yielded

Research and Analysis
- Analyzed
- Assembled
- Assessed
- Audited
- Calculated
- Evaluated
- Examined
- Forecasted
- Identified
- Interpreted
- Investigated
- Mapped
- Measured
- Qualified
- Quantified
- Surveyed
- Tested
- Tracked

Regulation
- Audited
- Authored
- Blocked
- Delegated
- Dispatched
- Enforced
- Inspected
- Itemize
- Screened
- Scrutinized
- Verified

Written or Oral Communication
- Authored
- Briefed
- Campaigned
- Co-authored
- Composed
- Conveyed
- Convinced
- Corresponded
- Counseled
- Critiqued
- Defined
- Documented
- Edited
- Illustrated
- Interpreted
- Lobbied
- Persuaded
- Promoted
- Published
- Reviewed
- Translated

Working
- Aided
- Assisted
- Collaborated
- Consulted
- Served
- Sponsored
- Supported
- Undertook
- Volunteered

One of the benefits of starting with an action word is that it can avoid one of the most common mistakes in resume writing: passive voice. Even though passive voice is not grammatically incorrect, it makes your resume longer than necessary and weaker in style. Passive voice occurs when the subject takes a secondary role in the sentence and is acted upon rather than doing the action. Some ways to correct these issues are:

- Start with an Action Word.
- Rewrite bullet points that sound like job descriptions.
- Remove anything that has not yet happened.

Let's take a look at a few examples:

Passive: A promotion to manager was awarded to me after only one year of service.
Active: Promoted to manager after one year.

Passive: 10% revenue growth was realized over two years by improving customer relations.
Active: Improved customer relations over two years, increasing sales by 10%.

Passive: Responsibility was recognized as one of my strengths.
Active: I am responsible.

Action Words

Passive: Responsible for forecasting customer trends by analyzing sales data.

Active: Analyzed sales data to forecast customer trends.

After you have chosen the words that define the actions of your position, you can start thinking of how to explain the actions. To help with describing your explanations, focus on one action word at a time and try to answer these questions:

- **What did you do?** Start with the action word. Try to avoid using the same action words throughout your resume. Use synonyms to add diversity to your action words.

- **Who was involved?** Explain who the important stakeholders and participants are. This should include others you worked with or the recipients of the action or product.

- **How did you do this?** Mention any specific tools or skills that were used. For example, if you developed a software application, list the coding languages you used.

- **Why should we care?** This is the impact or result of your actions.

Let's apply this to some of Brian's basic information boxes that we created in the previous chapter.

> ### Arabic Interpreter
> - **What did you do?** Served as an Arabic interpreter.
> - **Who was involved?** Fairfax County and 30 asylum seekers from Middle East.
> - **How did you do this?** Arabic – verbal communication
> - **Why should we care?** Facilitated verbal communication

> ### Arabic Translator
> - **What did you do?** Served as Arabic translator
> - **Who was involved?** Worked closely with the Newspaper Editorial Department in a collaborative manner
> - **How did you do this?** Arabic – written translation
> - **Why should we care?** Translated news articles, political cartoons, and Kuwait history
> - **What did you do?** Received a certificate of appreciation
> - **Why should we care?** Award for excellence in volunteer service

> ### Arabic Translator
> - **What did you do?** Served as a personal Arabic translator
> - **Who was involved?** Pastor of church
> - **How did you do this?** Arabic – verbal communication
> - **Why should we care?** Helped pastor communicate with Egyptian congregation
> - **What did you do?** Served as an Arabic translator
> - **Who was involved?** Egyptian congregation
> - **How did you do this?** English to Arabic – communication
> - **Why should we care?** Translated Sunday church service

As you can see from the examples, some of Brian's volunteer experiences did not have answers to all the questions or contained some repeated information. Even so, it's still a good way to check what information you want to include in your resume. The more detailed you are, the better, as it's always easier to edit out extra information than add it. Once you have all these written out, you can start rewording them into a complete bullet point, starting with the action word.

We combine the basic information from the previous chapter with our recently completed action word questionnaire. In addition to combining all the information, we need to format each of the sections so they are easier to read and more consistent throughout. Also, to further highlight Brian's Arabic skills, a skills section has been added to explain more specifically his ability in Arabic.

Due to the constraints of the size of this book, we are unable to add more details to each of the bullets or highlight other skills. If this were a regular sized resume, we might consider adding some of his previous work experience if he displayed the skills the position he was applying for desired. Experience such as training, mentoring, leading, or managing is obtainable in most jobs and might be worth mentioning.

Let's take a look at Brian's revised resume.

Brian M.
Vienna, VA | 703-200-000 | brian.m@example.com

Education

Bachelor of Arts, Global Affairs   **May 20XX**
George Mason University – Fairfax, VA
GPA: 3.2

Volunteer Translation Experience

Arabic Interpreter   **Dec 20XX – Present**
Fairfax County – Fairfax, VA
- Served as an Arabic interpreter for Fairfax County to facilitate verbal communication with over 30 asylum seekers from the Middle East.

Arabic Translator   **Feb 20XX – Dec 20XX**
Kuwait Newspaper – Kuwait
- Collaborated with the Editorial Department as an Arabic translator for roughly 30 news articles, political cartoons, and Kuwait history.
- Received a certificate of appreciation for excellence in volunteer translation services.

Arabic Translator   **Sep 19XX – Dec 20XX**
Christian Church – Vienna, VA
- Served as a personal Arabic translator for the Pastor on a weekly basis to communicate with Egyptian congregation of 15.
- Translated Sunday church service to Egyptian congregation from English to Arabic.

Language Skills

- Arabic (Egyptian, Kuwaiti, Lebanese) – Native fluency in speaking, listening comprehension, writing, and reading.

This is more like it! The resume passes the six-second test, and you can clearly glance over each section and find what you are looking for. The reader can see Brian is still in college pursuing a Bachelor's degree, and has quite a bit of translation experience. Even though his resume makes it clear his experience is voluntary, it still is valuable experience that should be considered for the position. The skills section also notes his Arabic fluency is native level.

In one of my resume workshops, I spoke to a group of Political Science students and asked them what kinds of careers were they looking to obtain after college. One of the careers was government work as an intelligence analyst. I then asked if anyone could tell me some of the essential skills are required of that profession. Eventually, we established writing, researching, and briefing/presenting were the top three. I then proceeded to show them an example of what a potential applicant may have in their resume to exhibit those skills.

Experience

Intern　　　　　　　　　　　　　　　　　　May 20XX – Sep 20XX
U.S. Department of State – Washington D.C.
- Collaborated with senior analyst on a European Economic Indicators Project and writing intelligence reports.
- Explored over 70 civilian organizations and institutions impacted by economic policy changes in Europe and compiled summary findings.
- Coordinated with three other interns, and briefed weekly economic highlights to senior State Department leaders.

Teaching Assistant　　　　　　　　　　　　Jan 20XX – May 20XX
East Asia Public Policy 201 – Virginia Tech – Blacksburg, VA
- Taught two classes of 20 students regarding public policy of east Asia countries on a weekly basis.
- Developed 25 lesson plans through directed research and collaboration with Political Science Department.

Research Assistant　　　　　　　　　　　　Sep 20XX – Dec 20XX
Virginia Tech – Blacksburg, VA
- Researched and interpreted hundreds of primary source documents from the Reagan administration through the Bush administration on nuclear proliferation in China and the Koreas.
- Generated over 50 summary findings on topics such as nuclear proliferation and terrorism using online resources and databases.

In this example, you can see that it not only displays experience in those three skill categories in some form, but it also shows the subject matter that is relevant to a government position as an intelligence analyst.

For technical positions, you want to show how you have used your technical skills. As a recruiter I have seen many resumes that simply just list technical languages or tools they know. While this might work for an ATS, a list doesn't give much insight into an applicant's proficiency or expertise in those technical skills. Let's take a look at an example of how we can mention technical skills and how they were applied in a work setting.

Experience

Software Developer   Jan 20XX – Present
SampleTech Inc. – Brooklyn, New York
- Led a team of five developers in creating a full-stack application for a financial institution using Java, Angular, HTML, CSS, and SQL.
- Developed weekly and monthly Tableau dashboards to help forecast projected earnings for executive level management.

Applications Intern   May 20XX – Aug 20XX
TechCompany – San Jose, California
- Wrote over 50 test cases in Junit for a Java backend application regarding patient health data.
- Created python scripts to filter through SQL database with over 5000 records of patient data.

Web Developer Intern   May 20XX - Sep 20XX
Startup Sites – San Francisco, California
- Designed and Developed websites for two educational institutions using JavaScript, HTML, and CSS: www.educationSite.edu and www.educationSite2.edu

---

To point out a few things this example displays:

- Experience leading a small development team in creating a full-stack application.

- Explains how Tableau was used for executive level

management.

- Displays the type of data that the individual has worked with – financial and patient data.

- Links to the websites that were created is another way to allow the recruiter to view a work sample.

Placement and Order of Importance

Growing up, I always enjoyed playing chess. I'm not an expert by any means, but I did have the chance to play a game with a chess prodigy. Naturally, within a few quick moves I was finished. While I personally don't enjoy losing, I made the most of it and asked for advice on how he played the game. The prodigy explained that he thinks at least five steps ahead and anticipates his opponent's moves. After considering what he'd said, I asked if I could play him one more time. Even though I lost easily a second time, I was able to last a bit longer because I was thinking further through my strategy.

The order of your moves is vital to winning the game in chess. Similar to chess, placement is important in capturing the attention of a resume reviewer. A human reader will only give your resume a few seconds. There are a few things that can help the recruiter go through your resume.

Reverse Chronological Order
Your experiences should be in reverse chronological order. This is the standard way to present your experience in a resume and is expected. A recruiter will want to know what you are doing in your current or latest position. Having your

experiences in reverse chronological order can also help tell the story of your growth. I have seen numerous resumes where an individual started as an intern in a particular field. Later, they worked in a few relevant full-time positions. Then finally took a lead position or more senior position in that field.

Position Titles Supersede Company Name
When reviewing resumes, I value the position title over the company name. I want to know what you did rather than who you worked for. A prestigious or well-known company may look good on your resume, but it carries very little weight if what you did was not relevant to the position you are applying for. By making your positions more noticeable than the company name, a recruiter can quickly scan your resume to see if your experience consists of positions that are relevant. Additionally, make sure that the reader can easily understand your job titles.

Section Placement
I have consulted with several individuals who wanted to make a complete career change. Their previous experience had little to do with the industry they wanted to move into. Because of this, I explained that they may want to change up the order of their resume to start with a section that highlights their relevant education, training, or certifications that they have completed or are in progress. Other sections that should be near the top are a skills-based experience section to highlight

relevant skills rather than a traditional reverse chronological work experience section, which contains experience that isn't relatable to the desired position.

One such individual had majored in Psychology but wanted to move into a technical career. He understood that he would need to start somewhere and was okay with starting in technical support. In order to move into an entry level tech support role, he needed to show he had the qualifications even without formal work experience. We took a look at a few tech support positions and found that many were looking for support for Windows operating systems and network devices.

I then asked if he had taken any formal training or had familiarity with any of the items listed in a personal setting, if not in a professional one. We then started to write down these items in a topical manner. We also had another section that listed technical certifications he had obtained or was currently working on. For placement, I explained, he may want to move the certification section to the top of his resume if the position he applied for listed any of the certifications as a hard requirement.

Technical Support Experience

Operating System
- Installed Windows 10 on five computers for friends and family, using USB installation.
- Used remote desktop to remotely troubleshoot family member's computer.
- Partitioned hard drive to allow for dual boot of Linux and Windows.

Network Installation
- Installed TP-Link, Tri-Band router and secured network using WPA2 with AES security for friend.
- Setup a personal Google Wi-Fi mesh network.

Malware Removal
- Used Symantec tools and tech forums to successfully remove trojan from friend's computer and preserved 100% of personal data.

Technical Certifications

CompTIA A+ Certification   October 20, 20XX
- Independently studied and passed certification

Network+ Certification   In Progress
- Estimated completion: May 20XX
- Independently studying and working towards certification

While not perfect, the above example is a start in the right direction for a skills-based resume. Even though nothing can replace relevant work experience, this example does show capability and potential in technical support.

Bullets

After writing your experience bullets down, see what the more impressive points are and rearrange them from most notable to least notable. While this may be subjective to you and the reader as to what is deemed more important, allow others to look over your resume to see what stands out to them. However, if the job description requires certain skills or experience, see how you can make them more apparent in your resume by placing them near the start of each experience entry.

Quantify, Quantify, Quantify!

When writing resumes, individuals often leave out quantity in regards to what was accomplished. When numbers are left out, the reviewer is unable to perceive how much of an impact you have made. One of the worst things you can do is simply write the job description in your resume. This is not a good idea because it does not specify to the reviewer what you actually accomplished other than the bare minimum job requirements.

If all you did was fulfill your exact job description, it shows you are average. Employers are not looking for average. They want individuals who are above average and can contribute more than what is asked for. In order to be competitive, set yourself apart from all the other "average" applicants who applied to the position and tell them what you have accomplished.

One way to determine if you can quantify your experiences is by asking questions. After writing an experience bullet, your bullet should be complete enough that the reader is unable to ask a question. Remember, it's always easier to cut information than add it. When trying to flesh out your experience bullets, try to see if you are missing details by asking questions. Let's take a look at a sample experience bullet.

- Prepared patient processing reports.

Yes, the above is an actual example of an experience bullet from a resume I have reviewed. The experience bullet is generic and leaves out a lot of information. Looking at the experience bullet, if you were looking to hire this individual, what else would you like to know? The questions I came up with are the following:

Quantification Questions

- **How many people was this for?** A quick way to improve an experience bullet is by answering this question. The answer to this question helps the reader gain a sense of scale. This is especially important when you have led a team and are applying for a position that requires leadership experience.

- **How often was this done?** This helps explain if this was a routine duty and perhaps how consistent you were in your efforts.

- **How much time was saved?** Answering this question helps define impact. Any time you can provide a solid impact with your contributions, it speaks volumes as to what you have accomplished in a previous position.

    Some other related questions to think about:
    o   Why are these reports important?
    o   Did these reports do anything for the company?

Other questions (not quantifiable, but still good to know):

- **Who were the reports for?** Sometimes the customer should be highlighted. If you prepared a product for executives or multiple departments, it can showcase the importance of your work.

- **What kind of patients?** This might be important to help give clarity to what you were doing. While this might not be necessary, it does give more detail to the reader.

- **How did you do this? What tools or techniques did you use?** If you use any specific tool or methodology that the position requires, showing how you applied it can provide more context to your experience level than just a list.

You may not be able to answer all questions for every single experience bullet you have on your resume, but being as complete as possible will vastly improve your level of experience and its impact. Let's try to improve our generic, sample experience by adding in some quantification.

> - Prepared weekly quality assurance reports for ten department heads, that helped reduce 25% turnaround time in daily patient triage for three Hospitals in Miami, FL.

Now this is an experience bullet! We now gain a sense of the scale of how often this report was prepared and who it was for. This also explains what the report was about—a quality assurance report. Most importantly, we now understand the importance of these reports. We have had an impact—we helped reduce the triage time for patients at three hospitals by 25%.

To reinforce this concept, let's look at a few more examples.

> - Coordinating with multiple departments, faculty, and students through the utilization of email, Google Suite, and Microsoft Office programs.

The above example lacks specific numbers, which weakens and generalizes what was done. The reader does not gain a sense of the scale of what was accomplished. An even greater issue is that the purpose of the coordination efforts is missing. Finally, the listing of technical tools is also weak, as these tools are too basic and general. Let's add some quantification and a purpose.

> - Coordinated with 30 faculty members across five academic departments to organize an orientation session for over 200 students.

The improved example's quantification provides a sense of scale on how many the individual worked with and for what purpose. Most important is the purpose – organizing an orientation session for an impressive number of over 200 students. Since the tools were too general and basic, they were removed to focus on what was accomplished and the impact.

> - Identified and maximized sales opportunities, and increased customer retention rates.

In this example, the reader is left wondering "how" sales were maximized and "how much" customer retention rates increased. Another issue is that there are two different experience items that may or may not be related. The bullet alone does not clarify if identifying sales opportunities led to an increase in customer retention rates. If they do not relate, these should be two separate bullets. For simplicity's sake, let's assume they are related.

- Analyzed sales data using PivotTables and developed loyalty program to increase customer retention rates by 40%.

With the new experience bullet, we now have one continuous experience that tells a more complete story. The addition of a specific skill to a tool is also introduced – "PivotTables." We also have more insight as to what the individual did (develop a loyalty program), and we have our impact quantified by a 40% increase in customer retention rates.

Format and Readability

In a previous position, I served on a working committee that was to think of new ways to improve the workforce. One of our primary objectives was to find ways to boost employee morale. As part of this committee, I led the organization of various events, from mentoring sessions to cultural events.

One of the biggest events I took charge of was planning an event to celebrate Asian American Heritage Month. The purpose of this event was to get people from other departments in the company to interact with each other, build networks, and strengthen relationships. One of the major challenges in planning such an event was ensuring effective communication so that everyone knew when to attend and what to anticipate.

The first email looked like the following:

Hello Everyone!

On May 15th, we plan to have an Asian American Heritage Month Event from 11:00 AM-1:00 PM in Conference Room 240. We will have the pleasure to hear from a special guest speaker, Ms. Susan Chen, regarding how her culture has helped her become a better leader in the workplace. Refreshments will follow. Please RSVP for this event by May 1st so we may adequately prepare for it.

After the first week, I hardly received any responses. I then realized that my email was too plain, and the most important pieces were buried under superfluous information. I then changed the format and organization of my email. I simplified the email and ended up with the following:

Asian Heritage Month Event
    What: Cultural Heritage Speaker Series
    Who: Speaker - Ms. Susan Chen, CFO
    Theme: "How Culture Enhances Leadership"
    When: May 15th from 11:00 AM – 1:00 PM
    Where: Conference Room 240
Refreshments and networking event to follow.
Please reply to RSVP for this event by May 1st

These changes to my initial email were well-received, and I had a much better response to RSVPs for the event. This resulted in a huge turnout for the event, gaining me praise and recognition from the seniors of the company.

Take a look at your resume and see if your formatting allows a reader to easily find anything. To help with format, you can apply a few mechanics that can help increase readability.

- **White space:** There should not be any paragraphs or large blocks of text.

- **Typographical emphasis:** Make use of bold, italics, and underlining to highlight different sections, titles, or separate information.

- **Bullet points:** Use bullet points to emphasize separate experiences or a list of skills. Each experience bullet point should be no longer than two to three lines.

- **Color:** Unless you are applying for roles like graphic design or something that requires professional visuals in some form where you want to display a skill in color use or formatting, keep your resume simple. Black font on white paper is the safest choice. Especially if you submit a digital resume where an ATS will scan it, unique formatting and color may not translate well.

Readability

If you want your resume read, you want to ensure that those reviewing it can easily understand its content. Sometimes we think using a bigger word or extravagant language will make us sound more intelligent. Remember, this is a resume, not a research paper. Recruiters are primarily interested in facts: Can you do the job? And what experience, skills, knowledge, and abilities qualify you for the position? The easier it is for a recruiter to see this, the better. Do not overcomplicate things.

One such tool you can use to determine the readability of your resume is called the Flesch-Kincaid Grade Level. The Flesch-Kincaid Grade Level is a formula that takes into account the length of sentences, total words, and syllables in a piece of writing to determine a reading grade level. There are several tools that you can find on the internet to evaluate your resume's readability.

In fact, Microsoft Word even has a built-in feature that can provide insights into the reading level required to comprehend your resume. The higher the grade level, the more complicated your resume is. If you find your resume is at an advanced grade level, you may reconsider rewording or shortening your sentences. For a resume, a safe target to aim for is an eight-grade reading level. Additionally, for optimal readability, try to limit each bullet point to two or three lines.

Chapter 5: Strengthening Your Resume

Jargon, Space Fillers, and Generics

With any profession, if you don't love it or lack passion for the field, career fulfillment is difficult to achieve. As a software developer for most of my career, I recognized early on the importance of staying updated with new technologies, practices, or methodologies. A constant drive to remain current with technological advancements is vital for success. This same drive enhances capability and competence in any role.

I understand that not everyone has a technical background or, more importantly, even an inclination for technical discussions. When people inquire about my job, I sometimes get excited and dive into details about a new tech trend that I started researching or how I worked on a new Python script to help automate a process at work. Many times, I will see the poor soul who asked about my profession begin to look around for an escape and nod as if only partially listening. I have a feeling that many of you reading this now are wondering when I am going to get to the point.

A common mistake in resumes is adding too much detail. Often times, we may include extraneous information that, while we may think it important and interesting, is boring to the reviewer. In many cases, the reviewer may not be able to figure out why such emphasis was placed on those details. It's essential to remember that a resume's primary goal is to secure an interview, not to serve as an exhaustive account of one's career. Save stories and details for the interview.

For example, I once reviewed a resume for a recent Ph.D. graduate looking to transition from academia. Her resume was filled with acronyms, terminology from her research, and spanned several pages. It resembled a research paper more than a resume. I explained to her that I had no idea what half of the things she had on her resume meant since it was focused too much on her niche research. I also explained that what she had was a CV, not a resume. It was doubtful anyone except an expert in her field would understand what she was trying to convey. To convert her CV into a resume, she would need to cut back on the jargon and extraneous details.

You will most likely not know who will be reviewing your resume. Often, recruiters are not experts in your field and might not comprehend the acronyms or jargon you use in your resume. Sometimes a recruiter is only given a short description of the job or a list of skills and qualifications to look for and may have a basic understanding or idea of what the job requires. While the recruiter will recognize common acronyms and language, a resume can become difficult and even tedious to read if you bury it in very technical language or terminology that is too deep into the subject matter.

It's unfortunate that in academics, at least in the US, students are often given assignments and research papers with minimum page requirements. This forces students to develop habits of stretching sentences and overusing passive voice to meet this minimum requirement.

However, when crafting a resume, less is more. You will want to find simpler ways to convey a point or explain your qualifications. Go over each of your bullets and see if you can say the same thing but with fewer words or using simpler synonyms. Here are a few examples of how to simplify:

- A substantial increase → Increased
- Acquired knowledge → Learned
- Utilized → Used
- Brought customer complaints to quick resolutions → Resolved customer complaints

I sometimes receive a military or government staffer's resume that is full of military terminology or acronyms. Even if you believe your intended audience would understand your

Jargon, Space Fillers, and Generics

resume's jargon, there is a great chance someone reviewing your resume will not be able to understand what you have written.

- SME in CO-IPE MA review and provided support of INDOPACOM COA and US CYBERCOM J3 in development and planning training program.
- Wrote and edited administrative publications for TSL staff using proper S&T and TSL guidelines.

These examples are hard to follow without having all the acronyms or titles explained. Try giving your resume to someone who doesn't know your field and see if what you wrote makes sense. If not, try to find a way to make things clearer and reduce the position/company specific jargon in your resume.

Remove Space Fillers

I have seen some resumes of individuals who felt that they needed to fill up all the space on the page. This can stem from a perceived lack of experience or wanting to portray that their resume had more substance than it actually contained. To stretch out the content, they sometimes add information that's neither necessary nor relevant.

The resume should only be about you, and it should be relevant to the position you are applying for. Because of this, you do not want to fill the resume up with references or extraneous or outdated information. Take a look at your resume and see if you have any of the following and remove them:

- **Photos:** Unless the job requires a picture of yourself (modeling, acting, etc.), refrain from adding any type of photos. The reason for this is to reduce bias. Whether the recruiter means to or not, seeing a picture of you will result in some type of bias. Also, photos can take up valuable real-estate on your resume.

- **Large section headers/dividers:** Section headers and dividers should not be overly large. While your name needs to be visible at the top of the resume, it should not overshadow the content. The primary role of headers is to demarcate various sections, so they shouldn't consume excessive space. Typographical emphasis will help with this. If your resume is running over a page, adjust the size of your header and section dividers and see if you can increase your resume's real-estate for content.

- **References:** The resume is about you and not anyone else. Leave out names of other individuals, their titles, and their contact information. It's also understood that a reference, should it be needed, can be provided later.

- **Company/Organization descriptions:** If recruiters are interested in what kind of company you worked for, they can do their own research or ask you directly about the company. The focus of your resume should be on you and what you accomplished rather than on the companies or organizations you worked for.

- **Outdated achievements:** Once you have a college record, there is no need to mention high school achievements. As you establish a professional record, start removing previous educational achievements, leadership positions in extracurriculars, and other academic accolades. Leave out any expired or outdated certifications. If a certification is relevant to the position but has expired, it may pose a question about whether you are current in your skills and abilities or up-to-date with the latest trends or regulations.

- **Unnecessary numbers:** Hours worked per week and salary should be left off your resume as they are all extraneous information. Mentioning salary can also cause an unintended bias. A high past salary might give the impression that you're too costly, while a low one might undervalue your worth.

- **Listing soft skills:** As explained earlier, remove lists of soft skills and other intangibles. Instead, show how you've applied these skills in real-life situations.

- **Self-rated skill charts:** The following is a sample of a self-rated skills chart:

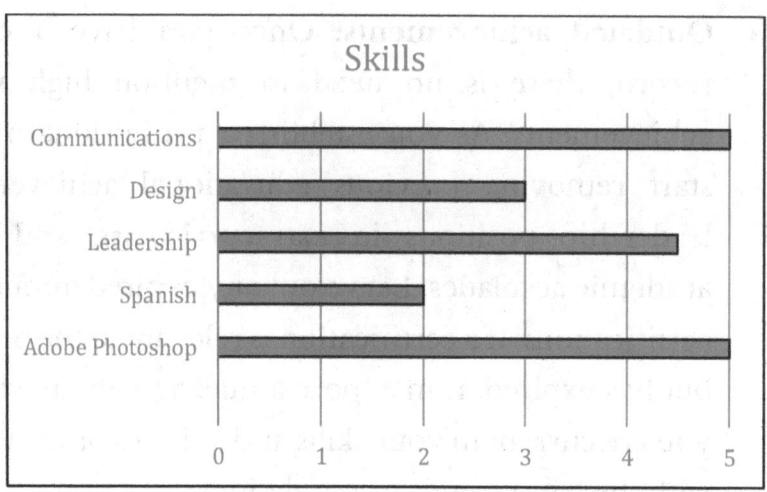

There are a number of reasons why these charts should be removed from your resume.

   o The chart contains an arbitrary point system with no explanation, meaning, or comparison.

   o Soft skills and other intangible skills shouldn't be rated on a point scale. Showing how you have applied them will be far more compelling than any point system or chart.

   o Even though a foreign language can be rated through a proficiency exam, this chart lumps different skills together that are unrelated. It also does not explain the proficiency level or what rating system you are applying.

- Instead of merely listing a technical skill, explain how many years of professional experience you have with it.

- Charts can take up a lot of space on your resume.

- Such charts may not be compatible with Applicant Tracking Systems (ATS), making them potentially unreadable.

Remove Generics

I have reviewed numerous resumes that start with an objective or an introductory paragraph. While some objectives may have some useful information, it is often buried beneath a lot of extra subjective and generic information. Such sections can also evolve into vast text blocks, consuming an unnecessary amount of space.

Let's take a look at one example.

Objective

Motivated and dedicated professional with years of experience handling multiple state organizations. Highly motivated and skilled individual with a Bachelor's in finance. Detail-oriented, analytical thinker who thrives independently as well as collaboratively.

This objective is fairly broad and generalized, and it leaves out details that I would want to know as a reviewer. For example, how many years of experience does this individual have? How large was the organization? Also, there are many soft skills mentioned. Merely citing these skills does not prove or validate that you actually have these abilities. Anyone can claim to have them. Whenever I come across such generic objectives, the first question that comes to my mind is, "How can you prove it?"

Similar to an objective, an introduction is also unnecessary. Let's take a look at an example.

Introduction

Tim is a Data Scientist with research and development expertise in applied artificial intelligence and machine learning programs for distributed and cloud computing. Tim is an expert in data analysis of medical data. He is a leader, self-starter, and team player.

This introduction seems rather generic, particularly the final sentence, which contains multiple broad, self-promoting attributes. While there is nothing wrong with these characteristics, anyone can list them. When I see broad statements such as this, I invariably think, "How can you prove it?"

Other than having similar issues to an objective statement, the introduction presents an additional challenge: it's written from the third-person perspective. When I see introductions like this, I often wonder if the resume was written by someone else. A resume should be a representation of your voice, articulating your experiences and aspirations in your own words.

Framing it in the third-person makes it sound like someone else is petitioning for the position on your behalf. I believe such an approach seems to undermine your position when you're the one actively seeking the role. From a recruiter's standpoint, if I'm considering hiring you, I'd rather hear your personal reasoning for being the right fit, not someone else's.

Professional Highlights

Okay, so we've established that statements of Objective and Introduction can often be too broad, too wordy, and too subjective. What can we do in place of these? If you have an established experience record, I would recommend starting a resume with a *Professional Highlights* section. This section will serve as your intro or summary. However, rather than a big block of text, this should be in bullet points, focusing on three to five items that truly highlight what you can do or have accomplished.

Professional Highlights

- Served over nine years as a professional instructor specializing in Social Studies and English for middle and high schools.
- Created and led students in over 50 activities and simulations of major historical events that allowed them to apply critical thinking and problem-solving skills.
- Developed curriculum for over 200 high school and middle school students.

This serves as a good example for several reasons:

- All points are in bulleted format. This layout is far more scannable than a dense paragraph, allowing readers to quickly digest and comprehend the information.

- Highlights only the major milestones of their career.

- Sticks with only factual statements rather than generic subjective ones.

- Quantifies experience to give a sense of the scale of what the individual has done.

Grammar, Spelling, and Mechanics

One of my favorite classes back in college was Business Writing and Communications. To my surprise, we began the semester with a spelling and grammar test. This test wasn't challenging in terms of concepts; instead, it highlighted common mistakes that many people make.

We spent the first few weeks of class just revisiting basic principles and concepts that many of us had either forgotten or never truly grasped. Granted, in today's world, we have auto-correct for spelling when we text, and applications such as Microsoft Word have become rather capable of correcting grammar mistakes. But relying too much on these tools can lead to embarrassing mistakes in the end, since they are not perfect.

I once attended an IT Security conference that had many amazing speakers. Many spoke on interesting topics, such as the latest hacking techniques used by criminals or security vulnerabilities that were recently discovered. One speaker was very energetic and had some great examples of his topic. Although he was good at speaking, he had numerous spelling errors on many of his slides. These errors served as a distraction and undermined his credibility.

As a recruiter, I have reviewed thousands of resumes.

Because of this, I have plenty of practice reading resumes and scanning for the information I am looking for. Errors, however, are glaring anomalies that immediately jump out as I read. If a position I am trying to fill requires "attention to detail," and I see a simple spelling mistake or grammatical error, it's immediately placed in the trash. Sounds harsh, right? Well, if I am looking for the most qualified applicant, I would expect them to be capable of submitting a resume that is free of typos or simple mistakes.

- **Practice makes perfect:** One exercise I recommend is spelling out words fully in your text messages. I understand the point of text messages is to communicate as quickly as possible, but taking the time to spell things out properly can be beneficial practice. Since much of our conversation via text is reduced to slang, acronyms, or even emoticons, we as a society have regressed in our communication skills. We're abandoning written language and moving toward expressing our thoughts in slang, symbols, and pictures. This may be fine in social settings, but not in professional ones.

- **Read out loud** - Another way to find spelling or grammar mistakes is to take the time to read out loud what you have written. When we write something down and silently read it to ourselves, we do not always pick up on how it actually reads because we often subconsciously correct mistakes as we go. When you read out loud, it prevents this subconscious auto-correction, and gives you a better sense of how your sentences flow. If you're finding it hard to read, then it probably needs revision.

- **Have it reviewed:** Sometimes you need a fresh pair of eyes to review what you have written. What may not be apparent to you, might be glaringly evident to someone else. Have a friend, colleague, or even a professional view your resume before you submit it. Sometimes they will be able to find errors that were not apparent to you.

Pitfalls and Common Mistakes

In basketball, when a team starts to pull ahead, they often gain what's known as "momentum." If left unchecked, they can continue to pull farther ahead until they have a lead that becomes almost impossible to overcome. The opposing team that is falling behind will try different tactics to stop the momentum. Timeouts or intentionally fouling the other team are used as a means to pause the game to prevent the opposing team from getting further ahead. These strategies break the momentum.

Similarly, when a recruiter reviews your resume, the last thing you want to happen is for the recruiter to pause and hesitate before moving forward in the hiring process. If there is something confusing, odd, or incorrect in your resume, there will be a break in the "momentum" of your resume's review.

During my personal review process, I've come across resumes that made me pause. One such resume was when I came across a software developer's resume that contained seemingly relevant work experiences and skills. Then I reached his skills line, which read:

Skills: Proficient in Java, HTML, CSS, Sequel, and C#...

One of the requirements for the position he was applying for was knowing Structured Query Language, most commonly known by its acronym, SQL. For those who are not familiar with SQL, it is often pronounced "sequel" but never written as "sequel."

Looking back at this applicant's resume and seeing this one line, I had to pause. The reason I paused was because it made me wonder why the applicant spelled it this way. Some questions came to my mind: Did he actually know SQL? Was he possibly faking it? What was the reason he spelled it this way?

Having to think of these questions broke my momentum in reviewing my resume. As I began to question his technical expertise, I resorted to my recruiter instincts: "When in doubt, throw it out."

Misleading the Reader or Misrepresenting Yourself

Early in my recruiting career, I came across a resume that had Ph.D. – ABD, listed under education. At the time, I didn't know what ABD stood for, nor did I really look into it. It wasn't until I was verifying the applicant's credentials that I found out this individual had not been awarded a Ph.D.

As I spoke with the applicant, I soon learned that ABD meant "all but dissertation," and the applicant had no intention of completing his dissertation as he was currently working fulltime. I then had to inform the applicant that the position required a Ph.D. and that we could not proceed further.

There's no argument that pursuing a doctoral degree or Ph.D. requires a lot of time, effort, and dedication. Some have advised that if you have done all the course work but have yet to complete a dissertation, you should still list it and have either the Ph.D.-ABD, Ph.D.(c), Ph.D.-c, or Ph.D.c (where the 'c' stands for "candidate").

However, more often than not, the person reviewing your resume will not be in academia. In my personal experience, whether it was intentional or unintentional, I felt that the applicants who listed either the ABD or c seemed a bit disingenuous of their actual credentials, especially when the qualification for the role required a Ph.D. A resume should be as clear as possible when a degree is still in progress. Remember, almost meeting a requirement will "almost" get you the job.

Similarly, another applicant's resume listed a master's degree in computer science, but when I had the opportunity to inspect his transcripts, it was actually a masters-in-passing; he hadn't completed his doctoral program. For those who are not familiar with this term, a masters-in-passing is a program that allows a student to pursue a master's degree concurrently with a doctoral program, and it's awarded along the way or at the same time as the completion of the doctoral program.

There are other programs similar to this, like Accelerated 4+1, which is a combined bachelor's and master's program that can award both degrees in a five-year program. In the case of the applicant claiming a master's degree, he actually had not yet been conferred the master's degree, as it was contingent on him completing his doctoral program. Since he had not completed his program, he should not have claimed a master's degree.

In any case, when listing degrees that have yet to be completed, it is best to be as transparent as possible and have clarifying language in your resume so as not to mislead an employer about your actual credentials. You can either clarify this in a cover letter or add clarifying language to your resume.

For example, in a resume, you can add the words "Anticipated Graduation Date" to clarify when you expect to complete your degree(s). This can help the recruiter know how to proceed when deciding whether to move forward with your application or not.

Leave Out Pronouns in Resume
When talking about yourself, the proper viewpoint is the first-person singular, "I." As an applicant, you are the only one applying for the job, not anyone else. You are writing on your own behalf and representing your experience and skills.

Whenever a resume is written in the third person, it not only reads differently but also feels as if someone else is speaking on the applicant's behalf. Your resume should be a representation of your voice. Something written in the third person should be reserved for writing on behalf of or advocating for someone else, such as a recommendation or a review. Leave out other pronouns in a resume.

Too Many Short-Term Jobs

This does not include Internships, as they are meant to be temporary and are good ways to acquire relevant experience. However, a slew of non-internship jobs that last only a few months may inadvertently display a lack of commitment. The last thing a recruiter wants to do is spend a ton of time getting an applicant through the hiring process and training, only to have them quit after a short time. This wastes a company's resources, time, and money.

To prevent this perception, take time to evaluate the reasons you want to leave a company before actually quitting. No job is perfect, but most jobs aren't so unbearable or toxic that you can't work for at least a few years. Building up your track record can also show your next employer that you can face tough situations and see projects through.

Numerous Time Gaps

Even if there are employment gaps in your resume, you do not need to provide an immediate explanation for them. As long as your other experience is relevant, the recruiter should not focus on the gaps. However, you do need to be prepared to answer any questions regarding gaps in an interview. Take time to practice what you will say.

Find a friend or mentor and ask them what they think of your response. In these situations, make sure you do not over-share personal reasons. A way to contain time gaps is to have a section that is clearly titled "relevant experience." Rather than mentioning all your work experience, this section would only provide the positions that are most relevant to the position you are applying for.

Chapter 6: Resume Extras

Career Fairs

Hopefully, by this point, you have a well-crafted "limited edition" resume. Now where else can you use your resume besides applying for positions? If you are still in college, you'll most likely have opportunities to attend career fairs. Career fairs are perhaps the best way to get face-time with a company, learn about opportunities they currently have, and potentially secure an interview for either an internship or fulltime position. Attending a career fair should be your top priority during your educational journey. You can be the most highly educated individual, but it's meaningless if you remain unemployed after graduation.

Often, several career fairs take place throughout the semester. Find out which employers will attend, the dates they will be on campus, and the types of positions they usually look to hire for. Take time to research which career fairs align best with your educational background and carefully plan out which employers you want to target. Sometimes, you might find multiple fairs that fit your field of study.

Understand that employers are coming to your campus looking for potential interns or new hires. You have a unique opportunity to engage directly with company employees and ask them questions about their company and the opportunities they have available.

- **Make a plan:** Each career fair has a set date and time. You may not have time to speak with all the employers, nor should you. Take time to plan out which employers are at the top of your list and prioritize which companies you want to interact with.

- **Prioritize:** Your education is undeniably important. But unless you plan on staying in academia, the opportunity to interact with a potential employer should take priority during your educational journey. If a career fair clashes with a class, work it out ahead of time with the instructor to allow yourself to attend the career fair. A good instructor should understand that the goal of an education is to help you gain knowledge and skills for employment and should not supersede opportunities to obtain them. Real-world experience is invaluable. One of my former professors wisely advised, "There is more to life than school."

- **Research companies:** Find out as much as you can prior to the career fair. The more time you take to learn about a company, the better prepared you will be when speaking with a recruiter or an employee of a company. For each company you want to work for, research what kinds of opportunities are available on the website—both internships and full-time positions. See what kinds of qualifications they are looking for. If possible, learn about the products and services they provide. Understand their company goals and the direction the company seems to be headed.

- **Bring copies of your resume:** A recruiter or employee of a company is your best resource to gauge how fit you are for a position. When I attended career fairs as a recruiter, I found it easier to advise potential applicants who provided me with a resume than those who came without one. Often, I have spoken to individuals who showed potential, only to find that they did not have a resume readily available. This matters because, even though some potential applicants are able to speak well about their qualifications, a resume can provide more detail.

During the career fair, there isn't a whole lot of time for a recruiter to thoroughly evaluate a potential applicant. However, an experienced recruiter will be able to use a resume to make a decision to either advise the potential applicant on anything that is missing or even decide to extend an invitation for an interview.

- **Bring project samples**: During one career fair, a student handed me a professionally created folder that had his resume, transcripts, and writing samples. What made this even more impressive was that his paperwork was all relevant to the position, showed good grades, and even the writing samples were well written. I was impressed with the extra effort he put in to be recognized and remembered. Needless to say, he was invited for an interview.

Going the extra mile to impress a recruiter will help you stand out among other potential applicants, as long as the contents are relevant. Ensure that not just the style (the way you present the content) but also the substance (the content you are providing) of your file are of high quality. If the previously mentioned student's folder contained an irrelevant resume, bad grades, or poorly written writing samples, the extra effort would have been a waste.

- **Have questions**: You only have a few short minutes with an employer. Make sure you do your research beforehand in order to avoid any questions you could have found out on your own. If you are waiting in line to speak with an employer, you may be able to listen to other questions being asked and the responses.

Come prepared with specific questions you really want to know the answers to. Try to avoid questions that are too generic in nature or something you could find out on their website.

- **Dress to impress**: While recruiters understand that you might have just come from class to attend the career fair, it doesn't hurt to make a good first impression and look presentable. Sometimes an employer may even have time to interview you on the spot or sometime during their visit. The interview section of this book will explain the importance of dressing appropriately for interviews.

- **Attend information sessions**: Employers will sometimes have information sessions during the week of the career fair. These are usually around an hour-long session that provides information such as an overview of the company, available opportunities, the application process, positions they are trying to fill, benefits, and time for questions and answers. The speakers are either recruiters or current company employees, these sessions offer insights into their experiences with the company, helping to clarify any ambiguities for potential applicants. If you are on the fence about applying to a company, attending these sessions might help you make a decision.

- **Be patient and observe:** During my college years, I attended several career fairs looking for employment. At every career fair, there are typically a ton of applicants for well-known companies. Often, I found myself waiting in lines before being able to speak with a potential employer. While there is usually a lot of noise and conversations going on, I learned that if I was patient and took time to listen, I could glean information while I waited to speak with an employer.

In one instance, I decided to wait near the booth and observe what was going on. I knew a little bit about the company, but I was curious to hear what positions they were trying to fill and what type of questions the recruiters were asking. While I waited, I heard the answers to some of my questions. I also noticed the recruiter asked everyone the same two questions.

  o Do you know how to write?
  o Do you speak a foreign language?

By the time I was able to speak with a recruiter, I was able to ask different questions and confidently answer the two questions the recruiter asked. Unless you know exactly how the company operates, take a more patient approach when first talking to them. Wait until a crowd forms and all the recruiters are busy talking to other potential applicants. Observe and listen in on what questions are asked and the reactions recruiters have in their responses. This can be especially effective if the company is very popular and you are waiting a while to speak with an employee or recruiter. You will appear better prepared and stand out from the crowd, an essential advantage for highly coveted positions.

- **Don't focus on swag:** Some of the nice things about career fairs are the cool swag that companies give out or other free items, but it's essential to remember your purpose. You have to make an impression. You're there to find out about the company as an employer. If you get some freebies, that's nice, but avoid being overly eager or making a spectacle of yourself. Employers are usually more than happy to give out what they have brought so as to avoid carrying any leftover items back, but don't make it the reason you go to an employer's booth. Take time to learn about the opportunities the employer has, as you may find a better opportunity that you had not previously considered.

Cover Letters

Often, a resume is paired with a cover letter. Cover letters give you an opportunity to explain why you want to work for a particular company and why you believe you're qualified for the position. A well-written and well-thought-out cover letter can significantly aid a recruiter in deciding whether to move forward with your application. However, a poorly written cover letter can have the opposite effect and hinder your chances.

Before drafting a cover letter, you should do your own research on the company and reflect on how your education/training/knowledge, skills, and experiences qualify you for both the position and the company. Make sure your cover letter is a single page, easy to read, clear, and concise. The goal is to convince the reader of one thing - Why should they hire you? To keep things simple, think of what qualifies you for the position, but delve deeper than what's already on your resume.

- Why do you want the position?
- What skills or unique experience set you apart from the other applicants.

Parts of a Cover Letter:

- **Header:** You can use the same header as your resume for uniformity or opt for a simplified version. Regardless, it should adhere to the guidelines outlined for the resume header earlier in this book.

- **Greeting:** If you're really ambitious, you can find out who the hiring manager is and address it directly to the individual. However, more often than not, this information is not available, or you could be completely wrong about who will see your cover letter first. Sometimes it's a recruiter who will be the one reviewing your paperwork first and not a hiring manager. Avoid using generic greetings such as "Dear Sir or Madam" or "To Whom it May Concern". Instead, "Dear Hiring Manager" is apt.

  Intro: Given the volume of resumes and cover letters that recruiters and hiring managers peruse, begin with a simple introduction of yourself and then state which position you are applying for. One of the sentences should outline the body of your cover letter. This sentence should contain your headers for the body section.

"I am currently an undergrad in Computer Science at Sample University and am interested in serving an internship for summer 2023 with SampleTechCompany. My educational background, technical skills, and relevant experience are the main reasons I would be an asset to SampleTechCompany."

If you are a mid-careerist or someone with more experience, you may want to begin your cover letter by summarizing your major accomplishments that are relevant to the position or expressing how many years of experience you have in the field. For example:

"I am a Software Developer with seven years of professional full-stack programming experience, served as a certified scrum master for over three years, and currently lead a web application development team of 10 at SampleAppCompany. I am interested in the Applications Developer Lead position, and believe my experience and skills suit the needs of your company."

- **Body paragraphs:** This is where you can go into more detail about how your skills, accomplishments, and experience qualify you for the position. Each topic you want to address should have a header to make it easy for the reader to scan.

- **Closing:** Keep this short. This can be a single sentence that wraps everything up.

    "I would appreciate the opportunity to meet with you to further discuss how my qualifications can assist your company in achieving their goals."

- **Ending and name:** End your cover letter with: "Sincerely", "Regards", or "Thank You" followed by your name.

Avoid the Following Issues:

- **Generic in nature:** Each company is different, so each cover letter should be unique as well. I've read several cover letters where the applicant recycled a cover letter for another company and forgot to replace the company's name. No matter how good the applicant was, I didn't read any further. If you're not taking the time to put in your best effort when applying, why should the hiring manager or recruiter take the time to read your cover letter or resume?

- **Spelling and grammar mistakes:** Make sure you thoroughly proofread your cover letter. Grammatical errors and spelling mistakes convey sloppiness and carelessness. Avoid slang and inappropriate language—maintain professionalism. Remember, this might be the first impression the company has of you.

- **Embellishment, misrepresentation, and lies:** As with any documentation you send to a potential employer, it is never wise to over exaggerate your knowledge, skills, abilities, or experiences. Do not make promises you cannot keep or make baseless claims that have no logical proof. Your integrity is worth more than getting any job.

- **Bringing up salary or benefits:** We all want compensation for our work, and the job posting should already give you an idea of what the position will offer. One big thing: you don't have the job yet. A cover letter is a written document that should speak only about you. Why even mention compensation or benefits? Save any discussions about compensation for after you have proven yourself as the best applicant for the position or if the recruiter brings up the topic. Emphasizing this in your cover letter hints at a primary focus on financials or benefits, which will not help your case.

- **Name dropping:** You are the focus of the application. When you name drop, the focus is taken off of you and onto the individual or company you mentioned instead. At this point, either the name is recognized or not. If the name is not recognized, you just wasted time mentioning an individual or company that the reader does not know. If the name is recognized, a few things can happen: the individual reading your cover letter may have a favorable, neutral, or unfavorable opinion of that person or company. With these odds, the name you mention will most likely not help you obtain a position. I have read several cover letters where the applicants mention a professor that they conducted research for, but often I have no idea who the professor is. They're not the ones applying—you are. As mentioned before, the cover letter should be about you and not someone else. More often than not, name dropping will be a waste of time and space.

- **Complaints or sympathetic pleas:** A cover letter is your chance to showcase what you have to offer. If you are complaining about an issue, explaining how unfairly you have been treated, or facing difficulties, you are missing the opportunity to show how you qualify for the job as this overshadows your qualifications. Avoid negative comments, such as complaints about previous employers, regardless of how true they may be. These stories will paint a negative picture of you.

If you have a disability, don't use it as an excuse for previous issues or special considerations. However, there is an appropriate time to ask for reasonable accommodations, but not in a cover letter. Bringing up disabilities in a cover story can unintentionally introduce bias.

- **Irrelevant details or too much information:** When a cover letter goes over a page, it can show the applicant doesn't understand what is actually relevant. Remember, the interview is the time to elaborate a bit more and give details. A cover letter is a small sample of what you have done, what you can do, and why you qualify for the position. Avoid using buzzwords or jargon that do not add value to the content of your cover letter.

- **Too much personal information:** To prevent bias, keep your cover letter professional. Do not include too much personal information. For example, talking about irrelevant topics such as hobbies that you do in your spare time or inappropriate subjects such as sexual orientation will not show how you qualify for the position.

Jane R. Smith

Orem, UT | (801) 100-0000 | j.smith@email.com | https://git.io/ZfzQ1

Dear Hiring Manager,   January 1, 20XX

I am currently an undergrad in Computer Science at Sample University, and am interested in serving an internship for summer 2023 with SampleTechCompany. My educational background, technical skills, and relevant experience are the main reasons I would be an asset to SampleTechCompany.

>**1. Educational Background:** I am currently pursuing a Bachelor's degree in Computer Science, and have taken course work that includes Database Design, Advanced Object-Oriented Programming, and Business Programming Logic where I have done collaborative software projects. I recently became a certified Amazon Web Services (AWS) Certified Developer.
>
>**2. Technical Skills:** I am experienced in several programming languages, including Java, Python, Angular, JavaScript, SQL, CSS, and HTML. I have listed a link to my GitHub repository which showcases several of my personal programming projects. I am also familiar with design principles such as Unified Modeling Language (UML) and User Experience (UX).
>
>**3. Relevant Experience:** I previously served an internship as an applications developer for DevCompany1. During my internship, I used Angular to update a frontend interface for a hospital's web application that provided patient information. I also followed test-driven development and wrote many test cases using Jasmine prior to writing my code. Additionally, I am serving as a teaching assistant for an introductory Java course.

I would appreciate the opportunity to meet with you to further discuss how my qualifications can assist your company in achieving their goals.

Regards,

Jane R. Smith

Resume Q&A

The following section contains questions individuals asked during some of my resume workshops for educational institutions.

- **Should we stick to one page or multiple pages?** For students, interns, or those at the entry-level, a resume should be one page. The only time it can be multiple pages is for a senior level position. Even then, the likelihood of anything being read beyond the first page is slim if the first page doesn't capture the reviewer's attention. If you decide to have multiple pages, the first page is the most important. However, if you are writing a CV, it is acceptable to have more than one page since it encompasses all previous academic and research history.

- **When should we remove high school activities from our resume?** Ideally, as soon as you have a college record. Remove them, especially if they are unrelated to the position you're applying for. Replace high school activities with college experiences or relevant personal projects. In the education section, once you have a college major and GPA, high school details become irrelevant.

- **How tied to government or defense events should we be if we are seeking a public sector position?** Your experience does not need to be in government or defense (even if that's what you're looking to have a career in or a position you're applying for), as long as the experience is relevant. However, directly relevant experience in a government position may give you the most credibility, as you are already working in that role and have experience in a position in the public sector. Non-relevant government experience may be helpful as it shows you have an understanding of how the public sector works, but it won't be as impactful. For any industry that you are working in, you should be aware of the latest trends, news, or current events.

- **Is it okay to list non-work experiences?** Yes, as long as the experience is relevant to the position in terms of desired or required qualifications. Experience can come in many forms. Look at volunteer opportunities, personal projects, or solving a problem to gain experience. Leave out experience that is not relevant to the position you are applying for.

- **Is it really more favorable to be bland in the format of the resume? Are those that aren't bland looked over?** The most important quality in terms of format is readability. Use the six second test. If you can find all the necessary information in a few seconds, then that format can work. There is always a risk with using unique graphics or special formatting if the company uses ATS software, as it may not be readable by their program. Remember, substance is more important than style.

- **How do I make my resume not look blank since I am a first-year student without much to put down on a resume?** While relevant work experience is best, the next best thing is having a section that can showcase personal or academic projects that can demonstrate your ability to do the job. For example, if you're interested in an analyst position, the main requirements are your ability to research, write, and be brief. On your resume, you can have a section that lists research papers you have written or presentations you have provided. If you have a long list of relevant work, suggest picking a few of your best works and a link to a portfolio that contains full samples of your work.

Other areas where you can add more depth to your resume are clubs, organizations, or volunteer work you have been a part of and the skills you used that are applicable to the position you are applying for.

- **Does it look good or bad to have a lot of student activities listed?** Only list student activities that are relatable to the position or display soft skills that are relevant to the position. Also, being a member doesn't tell the recruiter much. Look for opportunities to display skills the organization is looking for - leading a group, organizing an event, collaborating to produce...etc.

- **Do I need to list relevant college courses since I have to submit my transcripts?** Leave off course listings. The reason being that a recruiter will not be able to discern what is actually taught in that class. Also, recruiters aren't interested in what you learned but how you applied it. If the recruiter wants to know what courses you took, they can always request your transcripts.

- **I have a disability, should I mention it?** Your resume should focus on your experiences, skills, and qualifications. Mentioning a disability could lead to bias. Also, your disability should not define you. If you require reasonable accommodations, ask what the company offers and inquire about the application and interview process prior to applying.

INTERVIEWING

Chapter 7: Preparing for Interviews

The time was 6:55 PM. I patiently waited for my date, Amy, at a Sushi and Ramen restaurant. Since this was our first date, I wanted to make sure I was on time, if not early. Being five minutes early is always safe. By 7:10 PM, I began to wonder if Amy was even coming; she hadn't contacted me.

Around 7:15 PM, I finally see Amy walking towards me, her head down and eyes glued to her phone. It was clear she was texting someone. As she approached, she apologized—not for being late, but because she wanted to finish texting a friend! I probably should have ended the date then and there, but having travelled over an hour to meet, I figured I should at least give it a chance and see where the evening would go.

Once seated—and after she wrapped up her texting—we began getting to know each other. As we talked, I realized that every time I asked her a question, she would not make any eye contact. Every time I posed a question, her gaze wandered around the room but never met mine.

I soon realized that she was looking at her watch every few minutes. Later, she asked me what I was doing after the date. I explained that the date was what I planned for and that I was open to anything after. She then replied that she wanted to go rock climbing at 8:00 PM. I thought she was going to suggest we go rock climbing after dinner since she knew I, too, enjoyed the sport. But no invitation was extended.

Near the end of the date, Amy asked what type of person I was looking for. I explained some of the qualities I was looking for and then asked her the same question. She started to list what I considered unrealistic expectations, all with a tone and expression of "definitely not you". I then playfully let her know that even if such a person was out there, a relationship of any type works two ways. This person must like you as well. She then remarked, "But, I am AWESOME!" Needless to say, that was the first and last date I ever had with Amy.

Okay, you are probably wondering, "Why did I just read a story about a date? I thought this section of the book was about Interviewing?" or possibly "Why didn't you just get up and leave?!?"

On paper—or, in her dating profile—Amy seemed like a great match. But in person? The opposite. If I were the interviewer and she was the applicant, you don't need to imagine what the result would be.

Every encounter is, in essence, an interview. Regardless of whether the meeting is a date, a social gathering, or an actual job interview, each social interaction consists of at least two parties who make judgments and decisions based on the interaction. Ultimately, it is to decide whether to continue the relationship or not.

This section of the book is on interviewing. If you have an interview, or at least are on your way to preparing for one, then this part of the book will provide strategies on how to properly plan and prepare for them. The question for many individuals is, "How do I prepare?" If this is your first interview, preparation is even more important. While you may be comfortable talking to people, an interview is a different type of social interaction. The best way to prepare for any interview is to practice.

Perspective

At the start of my employment workshops, I kick things off with a simple game. On one end of a long table, I place a cup, and at the other end, a ball. Near the ball is a line of tape that splits the table in half. I then explain the rules.

1. Your goal is to get the ball into the cup without crossing the line of tape.
2. You have one chance.

I then invite a volunteer to try. Regardless of how skilled the player is, the cup is purposefully too small to have a ball tossed into it. The ball must be placed into the cup in order to win. So, how do you win at this seemingly impossible game? After the volunteer loses the game, I then explain the solution. I walk over to the table, remove the tape, and then place the ball into the cup. At this point, I hear a lot of remarks along the lines of, "If I knew that was allowed, I would have done it."

Have you ever played a game where you thought you knew all the rules, but in reality, you were making things harder on yourself because of your perceptions? Perhaps you would have implemented a different strategy if you had a better understanding of how things worked. When applying for jobs, an applicant will not have the recruiter's perspective prior to interviewing.

When you are invited to an interview, here are some perspectives to consider:

- **You met the qualifications on paper:** If you are invited to an interview just for submitting your resume, you met at least some, if not all, of the criteria the recruiter is looking for.

- **There are a limited number of positions:** Each recruiter has a limited number of positions they are able to hire for. It could be one or several. There could be other factors, such as different numbers of entry-level or expert-level positions available.

- **The recruiter may only be hiring in a certain geographic location or region:** If the company is nationwide or even worldwide, the recruiter only has a direct view and influence over the area they are recruiting for. For example, I went to a college in the mid-west. Most of the companies were hiring for the mid-west or west region, even though the company had locations on the east coast. When I tried to apply for an east coast location, even though my resume or application was sent to the recruiter in that area, I was at the bottom of the list, competing against applicants who had direct interaction with the recruiter in that area. If you have a specific area in mind for where you want to work, knowing what area the company is hiring for can aid in your decision-making.

- **The company is looking to hire someone**: No company has time to waste when recruiting. If you have an interview, it's the real deal, and there is a position available that you are being considered for. Companies don't interview for the sake of interviewing.

- **The interviewer may have filter/trap questions**: There may be some questions that are asked during the interview that are make or break questions. These are especially useful if the recruiter is on the fence about moving you forward in the application process.

- **The recruiter is on a schedule**: In some cases, a recruiter is on a deadline to fill a position. If you interview for a position and receive an offer, you may not have a lot of time to decide whether to accept. One thing to keep in mind is that you are most likely not the only one who interviewed for the position. If you take too long to decide, the recruiter may decide for you by moving on to the next qualified applicant.

- **The most skilled applicant doesn't always get the job:** Recruiters must consider a lot of factors when moving an applicant forward. You could be the top expert, but other attributes play a role in hiring decisions. Aspects like loyalty, integrity, cultural fit, growth potential, salary expectations, and personal likability are all part of the equation.

Confidence

A large part of an interview is how people perceive you. It's common to be nervous during an interview. However, if you are too nervous, it may prevent you from answering questions to the best of your actual ability. There are two ways to approach building your confidence.

1. Finding out what makes you nervous and working on it.
2. Finding out what helps you feel confident and using it.

Once you have figured out both of these, you can practice building your confidence for interviews. A confident demeanor can make your answers seem more credible. Confidence in your responses can convey to the interviewer that you are not only able to do the job, but do it well.

However, there is a fine line that you do not want to cross. You don't want to come off as arrogant or overly self-assured. Your choice of words and tone can significantly influence perceptions. For example, talking down to your interviewer or assuming you are the smartest person in the room about a certain subject is never a good idea.

A fellow recruiter once shared her experience

interviewing a young man who was dressed professionally and had a resume that seemed to fit the position well. Everything seemed to be going smoothly until he started to answer experience and situational type questions. During each response, he would spend time negatively describing his "incompetent" coworkers or how management didn't know what they were doing.

When asked about teamwork challenges he focused a lot of his response on disparaging his 'less than capable' teammates and how if it wasn't for his efforts, the team would not have accomplished the project. During the technical assessment questions, he asked the interviewer if she had any technical experience herself because he wasn't sure if she would understand his responses. She explained she would be fine and did not reveal that she had over 15 years of industry experience in the field, far surpassing his own. It's no surprise he did not get the job.

Practice Talking
In today's digital age, communication has shifted to faster, more convenient methods like texting. We are becoming busier and busier, and many feel they don't have time for long conversations. Because of this, we become reliant on technology to help us communicate, weakening our ability to communicate in person. The more you practice verbally communicating, the more confidence you will exhibit during an interview.

What is the Appropriate Attire?
After a day of multiple interviews with different members of an accounting firm, I had one last interview with one of the senior partners. I was dressed in a suit, and the first thing he said was, "Thank you for dressing appropriately! You are the first to dress in a suit!" I was kind of surprised at this and explained to him that I knew I was meeting a senior partner at the firm and wanted to dress appropriately.

We then spent a great deal of time having a friendly conversation about dress standards. We agreed that it's easier to dress down (e.g., remove a tie or coat) and almost impossible to dress up at an interview. Interestingly enough, that conversation ended up being pretty much my entire interview, and I was offered the job. Showing you are professional shows you are serious about getting the job.

Although many companies now lean towards relaxed dress codes, an interview might be the first time you meet someone from the company. It's always best to err on the side of caution and look your best. I have also never been told I was overdressed during an interview. As a recruiter, I am surprised at how often I am asked, "What is the appropriate dress for the interview?" My response is always the same: "It's an interview." To me, it should be understood that this means professional attire.

Dressing appropriately and having a neat appearance can help with confidence and show you want the job. While some may say dress and appearance shouldn't matter in an interview, this is an opportunity to display respect for the interviewer, show you are serious about the position, and prevent a feeling of inadequacy from feeling underdressed.

Take some time to understand the kind of company you are applying for and what kind of standards they have regarding dress. Even though employees of the company may dress casually, the big difference is that you are currently not an employee. The interview may be the first impression the company has of you. If you are uncertain what kind of dress standards the company has, ask someone. A mentor of mine once advised me, "Dress the part you want, then act the part."

Verbals and Non-Verbals

Once upon a time, I worked for Disney. Like many large organizations, they have an orientation to teach new employees about the culture, rules, and expectations. When I went through Disney's orientation training, I was taught how to appropriately treat guests at the various parks.

One of the lessons I still remember and continue to use today is how to point. The instructor explained that if you need to point, you must use two fingers or the entire hand. The main reason Disney taught this way of pointing was to avoid any offensive gesturing. I worked on this until it became second nature to me, and I still point like this to this very day.

During an interview, a gentleman would constantly point with his middle finger. I don't recall much other than remembering how he pointed. I know he wasn't intentionally giving me "the finger", but it was distracting nonetheless. I do remember thinking it was a shame he didn't have the Disney training I had. Sometimes we may not realize our non-verbal gestures may be too distracting, and that may be the only thing the interviewer will remember you by.

Other recruiters have told me about some of their most distracting interviews. An applicant who was so nervous she kept clicking a pen throughout the interview. While another continuously stroked her hair when she was thinking through a question. Unfortunately, neither applicant anticipated that their nonverbal tendencies would interfere with their ability to communicate effectively in the interview, detracting from their qualifications.

One strategy to mitigate as many distractions as possible is to place anything that you may fidget with out of reach during the interview, such as keys or jewelry. I also advise you to make sure your cell phone is off before the interview begins.

Appropriate Expressions
When my brother finished Physician's Assistant (PA) school, I attended his graduation ceremony. In the middle of the ceremony, they played a pre-recorded video from a graduate from the previous year. The PA explained how his education from this school has served him well in his current employment. He also shared a very somber experience about helping individuals in a third world country with a deadly disease and how it killed many of the patients he was trying to

help.

Apart from that, I don't remember any other details of his speech, nor do I remember what the reason was for telling this sad story. However, I do remember his facial expressions. He smiled at very odd intervals in the story. At the end of this sad story, he paused and smiled again. This is the main thing I still remember, and it was a little unsettling.

Similarly, in job interviews, you need to be mindful of your expressions when you tell your stories. The last thing you want to do is have any expression that acts as a distraction.

Seek Feedback

When I first started volunteering and teaching resume writing and interviewing, I wanted to make sure I was always improving and giving my best effort. At the conclusion of each class, I gave all attendees a survey. These surveys help me find out what is working or not in my lessons. After one of my first lessons, someone wrote, "The phrase 'you know' is used a lot."

In my next lesson, I was mindful of that phrase and caught myself a few times using it as a crutch to buy myself time, similar to the usual "uh" or "um". Because of the honest feedback, I was able to take corrective steps to ensure I was not using this phrase in my future lessons. After making these adjustments, I also felt more confident in my presentation.

You can and should solicit feedback from those you associate with as you practice your interviewing skills. Trusted friends, or even people you are meeting for the first time, can give an honest opinion of how you conduct yourself and also bring attention to phrases that you may rely on to stall or calm nerves. Practicing for a job interview is a must, and by asking for feedback, you can get a sense of what to work on.

While repeating certain words or actions occasionally might be overlooked, if done incessantly, it becomes problematic. You need to be self-aware and find ways to reduce these habits so they aren't distracting. The following are some questions you can ask when seeking feedback:

- What is the first and last thing you notice about me?

- Is there anything I do or say when I'm nervous?

- When answering questions, are my responses easy to follow?

- Do I go off topic or ramble when talking?

- Do I say or do anything when I am surprised or caught off guard?

Avoiding Bias

We meet new people every day. At an interview, you will meet individuals who come from different backgrounds. What you consider acceptable might not align with the perspective of your interviewer. Politics, religious views, personal lifestyle choices, and any other potentially controversial topics should be avoided during the interview.

The primary reason to sidestep these areas is the potential they hold to introduce unintentional bias into the conversation. During an interview, your aim should be to limit any potential biases against you. While interviewers should remain impartial, overriding personal biases can be challenging, as everyone is prone to them.

Bias is unavoidable. However, you can take measures to minimize it. Here is an example of a good response when asked, "Tell me about a time you worked with a difficult manager? What was your approach to the situation?"

"I worked for a manager who liked to micromanage. This individual would constantly ask for status update, and called me in numerous times to ask how I approached the work. I figured I needed to find a way to earn my manager's trust and prove I understood our processes and how to do my job. During a group meeting, my manager brought up issues regarding some of our manual processes. I took this as an opportunity and used my programming skills to create an auto-fill form and simplify the current process. This not only impressed my manager, but helped me gain credibility and trust."

This example is slightly generic, but I want to highlight my approach as it reduces bias in a few ways.

- **Gender neutral:** When you are talking about your experiences, you should get into a habit of removing pronouns like he/him/she/her/they/them and just use titles such as manager or colleague. This can prevent negative assumptions. For example, if you're a male and you explain a seemingly negative experience with a supervisor who is female, the interviewer may wonder if you have issues with supervisors of the opposite gender.

- **No names:** You never know who might be connected to the person you are talking about. Your view of an individual might be contrary to your interviewer's.

Once, a friend of mine was attending a business meeting for a new department in his company. Prior to the meeting, he overheard two of the workers making disparaging comments about a woman they had recently worked with and mentioning her by name.

After hearing their comments, my friend calmly remarked, "The woman whom you're talking about is my wife." Shortly after the meeting began, my friend was announced as the new director of the department. The two workers must have been mortified to know they had been insulting their new boss's wife!

- **No need for exact timeline**: Offering specific timelines can often be superfluous. Similar to naming individuals, telling exactly when an event occurred may reveal who was involved.

- **Keep things positive**: Negative responses give off negative impressions. If you must talk about someone negatively, especially a senior coworker or manager, make sure it ends on a positive note. To accomplish this, briefly mention the negative behavior or action. Then focus your response on how you resolved the issue or what you learned from the experience.

- **No extraneous information**: Sometimes we get nervous and start including or offering information that's unnecessary. Stick to answering the question and leave out details that don't add value.

Always bear in mind that the primary goal of an interview is to gauge whether your personal qualities—your experiences, character, knowledge, and abilities—are in line with the position for which you're being considered. One other important quality a company will look for is your ability to acclimate to the culture of the company—are you a good fit for the company?

Every company has a certain culture that may or may not suit you. Do your research and find out as much as you can about the company's culture before an interview. This will reduce any surprises you may face if you get the job.

Honesty and Integrity

A **company** I once worked for sought out individuals with foreign language abilities, especially in Chinese. It was a big deal when we hired someone who possessed both technical and language skills, as they could contribute a lot more than the average technical writer. One day, we had a new hire sent to our department. We heard she had some language ability, but we did not know to what extent. When she introduced herself, she explained she was fluent in Mandarin Chinese and touted her technical expertise.

After her introduction, many of us were eager to work with her because of her claimed experience. However, halfway through the day, it became evident that she lacked both the technical know-how and Mandarin fluency she claimed. She had oversold her abilities, and even though she was hired, none of us wanted to work with her. Thereafter, there was always a palpable distrust in her work.

Later, I had the opportunity to participate in a mentoring session with several senior partners of the organization. I asked each of them the same question, which was, "What is the quality that you admire the most?" Each of them gave the same response: Integrity. One of them even remarked, "Integrity is like your virginity. Once it's gone, you can't get it back!" The episode with our colleague served as a stark reminder of this sentiment. Once we knew that she had exaggerated her abilities, we were never able to trust her work or her word. That wisdom has since become a guiding principle in my professional journey, prompting me to always present an authentic account of my capabilities and work ethic.

Embellishing your experiences may seem like a good way to make you look more competent, but a perceptive recruiter will know when you are lying and will see through the facade. Even if you secure the job under false pretenses, the inability to deliver on your promises will only create issues down the road.

As long as you are honest about your efforts, you never need to worry about a recruiter finding out the truth. Never sell your integrity to get a job. If you do this, it will eventually show in your work and any of your business dealings. Once others learn of your dishonesty, it is almost impossible to rid yourself of that perception.

Rather than heading down the path of dishonesty, you should instead take time to find out where your actual strengths and weaknesses are. If there is a skill that the position requires, start working on it. Some good advice I was given is to not only continually work on the current skills that your job requires, but to also start working on learning new skills you need for the next position you want.

Best Effort

One of the more unique experiences of growing up in Orlando, Florida, was the opportunity to work at a theme park. One summer, I worked as a show host for one of the attractions at Universal Studios: "Earthquake and the Magic of Effects." The show has changed over the years, but back then, I had to memorize a script, with the show lasting about 15 minutes. Before being assigned, I was tested on my ability to basically act out the scripted dialogue word for word. The director of these types of attractions made sure it was word perfect.

I had a friend who was exceptionally talented at acting and tried out for the part as well. However, whenever she forgot parts or wasn't certain, she would improvise or deliver lines that were "close" to the original script. Despite her superior acting skills, this deviation from the script cost her the job. The strict adherence was because the show had to be the same for everyone visiting the attraction, and the best way for quality control was through verbatim dialogue.

While I wasn't the best actor, I was able to memorize the script word-for-word and was successfully hired as a show host. As one of the newer team members, I was paired with a trainer who had done the show for quite some time. My trainer explained that if I learned one thing from him, it was to make sure that I did every show as if it were my first and give it my all. There would be a new audience at every show seeing it for the first time, and they deserved nothing less than my best effort.

This experience highlights that every interview is different. Even though you may go through tons of interviews, often receiving some of the same questions, it's important to make sure that you treat each interview like it's your first. Now, I'm not saying to have the same type of first-time jitters or fears, but delivering your responses with the same enthusiasm.

Make the interviewer interested in you. Captivate their attention with interesting stories that you have experienced. Even if you've told the story a million times, the interviewer has most likely not heard it. Each interviewer will be different, and if you can make a positive impression on the interviewer, then you will have a better chance at getting the job.

Don't Waste Time

Nothing bothers me more than wasting time. Everyone's time is valuable, but recruiters spend a considerable amount of time vetting and sifting through applicants before offering an interview. Setting up and conducting interviews is also time-consuming.

I have had my fair share of time wasted from applicants who were actually not interested in the position. Some accepted interview offers merely for practice, to fulfill a class assignment, or were unsure and just wanted to "see what's out there." If the reason is anything besides actual interest in the position, it's best not to apply or agree to an interview.

- **The company's time and money are wasted.** If a firm is in the area for a recruiting event, they might have limited time. Similarly, there could be a cap on the number of interviews they can conduct. Interviewing a non-serious applicant wastes time that could have been more productively spent evaluating a potential new hire.

- **Your own time is wasted.** You should value your own time as well. Why interview with a company you're not interested in? Wouldn't it be a better use of your time to only interview with companies you really want to work for?

- **A real interview should not be used as practice.** If you're looking for practice, do a mock interview where you can get actual feedback. A real interview isn't the right setting for practice, especially since companies seldom offer comprehensive feedback on your interview performance. Even if they do it's usually very minimal.

- **It's selfish.** By occupying a slot, you might be sidelining another deserving applicant. How would you feel if there was a job you really wanted, but the company wasn't able to interview you because they were instead interviewing a non-serious applicant?

- **You may unknowingly contribute to a negative trend.** I recall recruiting for a college that seemingly hadn't emphasized the gravity of interviews to its students, or the importance of respecting employers' time. The company I recruited for was on the East coast, and since we were recruiting at a college located in the mid-west, one of the questions I made sure to ask, repeatedly, and before selecting any applicant for an interview was, "If offered a position, would you be willing to relocate?" We only had time for 10 interviews, and each applicant we selected for an interview said relocation wasn't an issue.

After an exhaustive day, we extended offers to nine out of the 10. However, seven out of these nine turned down the offer because they wanted to stay in the area, and did not want to relocate. The next year we decided not to return to this particular college and focus our efforts on ones where we had more success. Imagine if you were a student attending this college and fewer employers showed up at your college's career fair because of the reputation created by students in the past.

Chapter 8: Approaching Interviews

Prepare

When I first moved to Northern Virginia, I was unfamiliar with both navigating the traffic and more importantly, the traffic laws. For starters, I couldn't believe how bad traffic in general was in Northern Virginia. It's horrible! To make things worse, all the lanes on a particular highway change into High Occupancy Vehicle (HOV) lanes during a certain time of the day, and police officers station themselves at exit ramps, poised to ticket any violators.

Unfortunately for me, I made such a mistake and ended up with a ticket that was close to $200. Thank you, Virginia. As I reread the ticket and researched everything about Virginia laws on the HOV lanes, I unfortunately learned there is absolutely no forgiveness for ignorance.

I decided that even though I may not be able to plead

ignorance, I could figure out a way to get a more lenient fine if I could explain how unfair the whole ordeal was. I then gathered as much material as I could to persuade the judge of my "ignorance." By the time my court date arrived, I had in hand my Florida license plate, Florida driver's license, college transcripts, current housing documents, and even photos of the signs sourced from Google Maps.

When the judge called my name, he asked how I pleaded. I had no choice but to say "guilty". To make matters more daunting, the officer who had issued my ticket was present. After speaking to the officer, the judge asked me if I wanted to say anything. That was my moment. I then began by explaining everything I could. I explained how I just moved into the area, how for the past five years I was in college in a different state, and how for most of my life I had been a Florida resident. I even printed off images from Google Maps to show how confusing the signs were. The judge found my arguments convincing enough to dismiss my ticket.

Ultimately, I was lucky to have a nice judge. He had no reason whatsoever to give me leniency. He could have easily made me pay the fine and moved on to the next person. But my level of preparation impressed him. This experience showed to me that it's always better to be over prepared than under.

For those who have gone through many interviews the worst thing you can do is "wing it." Being prepared gives you an edge that can carry you through the difficult odds of being hired, and can improve your chances of the interviewer understanding your story and recognizing why you are the best applicant.

What to Bring in an Interview

- **Copies of your resume:** An employee of a company started our interview by introducing himself and immediately apologized, explaining that he hadn't had the chance to review my resume or know anything about me. Turns out he was a last-minute replacement for my original interviewer. I then asked him if he wanted to take a moment to look at my resume before we began. He agreed and I handed him over a copy of my resume. While I still gave a very short elevator pitch about myself, having the resume on-hand showed I was prepared and also allowed the interviewer more information about me.

  Always have a few copies of your resume on hand during an interview, especially when there might be multiple interviewers. It's also possible that some might not have had the opportunity to read your resume prior to the interview. In my situation, having my resume ready showed I was prepared for the interview. I also set the stage for the interview by offering a solution for the interviewer's lack of preparation. Rather than being upset that the interviewer was unprepared, I showed I could be flexible in the moment and understand that sometimes things happen.

- **Notepad and pen:** An interview is important for both parties. For the interviewer, it can demonstrate how prepared an applicant is. As the applicant, it's just as important to find out if the position is indeed what you are looking for. Remember, an interview is a two-way street. Throughout the interview, you may hear valuable information, such as instructions for next steps in the interview process. A notepad is useful for writing down key information that you may not necessarily remember later. Here are some ideas of information you may want to write down:

    o When will you hear back?
    o Is there another interview?
    - Where will the interview be held?
    - Who will the next interview be with?
    - What will the interview be about?
    - How long will it take?
    o Due dates of information or assessments.
    o How long is the rest of the hiring process?
    o Names of people you have met or will meet:
    - Interviewer
    - Recruiter
    - Human Resources
    - Managers
    - Working level Employees

o   Answers to prepared questions – Ask questions that can't be found through researching the company and write down the interviewer's responses.

- **Portfolio or samples of work:** Fresh out of college, I spent over three years in a non-technical role. I felt the technical skills I worked hard to obtain during college were being wasted. So, I applied for a position that was looking for at least three years of technical experience as a Java programmer in a professional capacity. I had zero.

However, for my master's degree, I had to develop an entire full-stack application for a software company, from design to prototype. I kept all the design documents, diagrams, and screenshots of both the code and interface. I decided to bring that along as a means to showcase my programming abilities.

During the interview, they asked if I had any experience in software development. That is when I brought out my project. I briefly explained the project, the steps taken, and the results of the project. Even though I did not have the three years of experience they were looking for, I was able to show them I could still do the job since I had the necessary skill set. In the end, my preparation paid off as I was offered the position.

Depending on the job you apply for, you may want to consider what type of work samples you can show to your interviewer. Make sure whatever you decide to bring is relevant to the position and can be easily understood or quickly explained. If it's too complicated or visually unappealing, it may actually hurt your interview rather than help.

Realize that the goal is to be prepared when the chance to showcase your samples comes. More often than not, you will not have the opportunity to show these samples. The idea is to have them on-hand if the opportunity presents itself. Some ideas of what you could bring if they are relevant to the position you are applying for:

- **Short writing samples:** If you bring writing samples, make sure they are formatted in a way that they can pass the six-second rule. In this case, if a person glances at the first page or skims the content, they know what the title is and perhaps what it encompasses.

- **Data visualizations or project reports:** This may not be possible due to company confidentiality, but if it's a report that you created on your own, such as a Tableau dashboard of some type, it might be worth showing. You can even give a brief overview of what it is, why you did it, who it was for, and the result/impact.

- **Diagrams or models:** Simple diagrams or models that are visually easy to grasp in a short span of time work well when used as a reference. Save the more detailed ones if they ask to look at them. Learn how to talk about your diagrams from various perspectives, depending on where the interviewer is seated. Be able to guide the interviewer through a part of the diagram.

- **Portfolio of graphics/artwork:** For any occupation requiring visuals, having a portfolio on hand is always a great way to be prepared to show what you can do.

- **List of references:** Employers will not ask for this during an interview, but it doesn't hurt to have this handy somewhere, as you never know what information they will ask for or when they will require it as you progress through the application process. As long as you have this list with you – such as a document on your smart device or an organized print-off – you will always be ready when they ask for it.

- **Presentation:** If one of the major skills of the

position requires the ability to give presentations, you may have an opportunity to showcase these skills with a short presentation. Keep in mind that you should keep this roughly no more than perhaps three minutes in length, as this should be a sample of how you present an idea, concept, or previous briefing.

- **Platforms**: There are numerous platforms that can host digital samples of your work. However, for an interview, ensure that the project you want to share is readily accessible, as you may not have access to the platform if there is no internet access. As a recruiter, when I interview applicants for a technical position, I require at least one sample of their work. It can be an academic, personal, or work project, as long as there is nothing sensitive or proprietary information. Seeing their project can help me evaluate them on a number of items, such as presentation ability, applied knowledge, and skill level.

Organize

Place all materials in a bag or small organizer of sorts that ensures any physical handouts/materials are not wrinkled. If these are on a device such as a laptop or tablet, make sure your device is fully powered and ready to use when you need it. Note that some companies may not allow you to bring your own personal devices. If this is the case, respect their rules and bring only what you are allowed to.

When I interview for a job, I use a laptop carrier that has separate compartments for documents, a notepad, and other supplies like extra pens and small breath mints (never use gum because chewing gum during an interview is distracting). Whatever you decide to bring, make sure everything is organized and easily accessible. The last thing you want to do is bring a bunch of materials and have trouble finding what you need at the time.

Provide Solutions

As an applicant, you can provide an innovative idea that can solve a problem or improve a process to impress the interviewer. This can display your desire to be an immediate contributor to the company and someone willing to go beyond the normal applicant. Even if the idea isn't quite viable, at least you are already thinking of potential process improvements and seeking to provide value to the company.

As mentioned earlier, interviews have a time limit. Because of this, you don't have a lot of time to explain a new idea. Regardless of the idea, rather than explaining everything, an overall summary of your idea and how it can work should suffice. This is not a guarantee that you will be hired, but this adds another element to your interview for the interviewer to consider.

A friend of mine used to work as a temp for a company. Near the end of her term, a full-time position opened up at the company. My friend not only wanted the full-time position, but her supervisor also encouraged her to apply for it. Not leaving anything to chance, my friend sought out my advice on how to best prepare for the interview. I asked her how long she had worked at this company and what she had done thus far. She explained that she had been working in the position for a little over two months and had the challenging task of revising the company's website.

Even though she was nearing the completion of revising the website and the term of her temporary position, there was other work that needed to be done. I then advised that she should bring an outline that detailed the changes she would make and included explanations as to why she would make those suggestions if she was in the full-time position. In the end, she created an organized one-page handout that outlined her ideas for changes and brought enough copies for everyone at the interview.

On the day of the interview, my friend brought her outline of improvements, handed each of the interviewers a copy, and presented her idea. The ones interviewing her were two other employees she had worked with before and her supervisor. Even though they already knew her and her work, she impressed them with her preparation, professionalism, and plan. They also remarked that they had never had a temp outline a plan of action that she would take if in a fulltime position. Needless to say, she was offered the full-time position.

Some companies use interviews as a means to generate

new ideas or find talent with different perspectives. There is always a risk in giving solutions where the company could potentially just take the idea and not hire the applicant in the end. However, if it's an idea that is simple and you're okay with the company using it, then you can give as much detail as necessary. Since the "loss" of the idea would not be a big deal, you can give low effort ideas easily. Either way, the benefits of sharing an innovative idea usually outweigh the cost.

Opportunities to share your idea may arise when you are asked a question along the lines of:

- Why do you qualify for this position?
- Is there anything else you would like us to consider?
- If you were offered this position, what would you do to innovate our processes?

Sometimes the opportunity to share your innovative idea might not present itself during the interview. If that's the case, your idea won't necessarily go to waste if you're offered the position. Also, your idea might prove useful in another context. It's never a waste to think of a solution. In my career, I have had many ideas that were never implemented. The ones that were used provided me with opportunities to advance in my career. It's always good practice to continually think of solutions to problems or ways to improve processes. You never know what impact your idea may have.

Interview Types

A crucial step in preparing for any interview is understanding what to expect. Since every employer is different, there are many different types of interviews that you may encounter. Here is a list of some interview types you may face.

- One-on-One
- Panel
- Virtual
- Phone
- Group

In the next few sections, we will delve into the more common interviews you may face. Since every employer is different, they may use one or a combination of interview styles throughout the hiring process. While this is not a conclusive list of interview types, it should serve as a guide to help narrow your focus a bit on what to expect during an interview. One thing to note is that even if you think you know what type of interview you're going into, always be flexible with whatever format of interview you are given.

In one interview experience, the company began with a timed skills assessment, followed by one-on-one interviews. For another company, I had multiple interview phases: the first was one-on-one with a recruiter, the second was a panel of my potential coworkers, and the final was with a managing partner.

Throughout all these interviews, the employers were purposefully vague about what to expect. They wanted to know if I could be flexible and adapt to unknown circumstances. Most of the time, while you might have an idea of the interview type, staying flexible will allow you to remain calm even during unpredictable situations. If you're too rigid in your preparation, you may lose focus and begin worrying about things that do not matter.

One-on-One Interviews

For one of my jobs, I had to take a language proficiency exam for Cantonese. The beginning of the exam consisted of a small conversation in Cantonese with a native speaker and would slowly ramp up in difficulty. Usually, when I meet someone for the first time, I try to say something to get the person to smile or get some type of reaction to help me get a sense of them and to see if we can relate to each other. When she asked me how I learned Cantonese, I half-jokingly replied, "through TV shows." The examiner showed no reaction to my response and gave me zero feedback.

As the exam continued, she continued to give no

expression to any of my responses. I felt this made the exam more difficult. Her lack of reaction also meant I wasn't sure how clear my responses were. In normal conversation, you watch the other person for cues on whether you are being understood, and can clarify as necessary. As the exam progressed, I decided to keep my responses serious and kept my usual humor out of the conversation. In the end, I did pass the exam, but I felt the entire experience was tougher since I was unable to get any expression from the examiner.

Three years later, I had to take the same exam from the same language center as a means to re-certify. Even though everything was the same format-wise, I had a different examiner. I began the exam as I had three years ago, explaining how I learned Cantonese mainly from TV shows. This time, my examiner chuckled at my response. As the exam progressed, I realized I was having an easier time as the examiner's reactions and expressions helped me know when my responses and tone were clear. I was getting the feedback I was hoping for.

One-on-one interviews are probably the most common interview type and one of the easiest to prepare for since they involve only one person. However, like my experience with the language exam, every interview is with a different person. While I had the same exam, since I was being evaluated by a different person in both exams, my experiences were completely different – I had to adjust my responses to fit the appropriate situation. Likewise, in an interview, you may have an interviewer who seems friendly and easy to carry on a conversation with. Contrastingly, another interviewer may seem like an enigma, making the interview more difficult. Either way, the focus of one-on-one interviews is the same: the individual.

In the introduction of the interview section, I mention how every interaction we have with someone else can be considered a type of interview. Naturally, the best way to prepare for a one-on-one interview is to talk to someone. The more people you talk to, the easier it will be to prepare for a one-on-one interview. If you are not comfortable talking to just anyone, start off with talking to people you already know, such as family, friends, or coworkers. For better practice, look for opportunities to talk to people you don't know, perhaps at social gatherings or while waiting in lines.

Practice telling stories. First, pick a personal story that you can potentially share during an interview. Begin with a friend, family member, or colleague with whom you interact daily. As you speak, practice eye-contact and observe facial expressions. If you notice bored expressions, then you may be adding too many details. If you receive many clarifying questions, you may need to add more details. The purpose is to gauge their interest level as you speak.

Next, try finding someone you rarely interact with and tell them the same story or experience. Even though everyone is different, see if you can get a similar reaction. Make note of the differences or similarities in their reactions or interest levels.

Lastly, repeat the same with a person you are not

familiar with or don't know at all. Opportunities to meet new people arise frequently—at parties, social gatherings, dates, etc. Keep sharing the same story or experience until it flows naturally.

Panel Interviews

Panel interviews can feel quite intimidating. It's a small version of public speaking, and you have everyone's attention. I remember my first panel interview being somewhat terrifying; it was in a large executive meeting room with nine individuals. I began the interview by shaking everyone's hand, looking them in the eye, and personally introducing myself to them. By doing so, I was able to get each person's name and position. As the interview continued, each team member took turns to ask me a question.

Regardless of who is in the room, when someone asks you a question, you need to talk to that individual first: the "asker." Since it's a panel interview, after addressing the asker, you should subtly turn to each member while you finish answering the question. Finally, when you are near the conclusion of answering the question, re-establishing eye contact with the asker.

Doing this does a few things. It first shows you are answering directly to the individual asking the question. Secondly, you are acknowledging everyone else in the room. Lastly, if you are quick, it lets you gauge everyone's reactions to your responses.

When the opportunity to ask questions comes your way, first address the interviewer who inquires, "Do you have any questions?" Your primary focus should then be on whoever responds next.

Don't forget to practice. Often at events, we gravitate towards those we already know or are already comfortable being around. By finding a group of people you are not too familiar with, you can practice your communication skills and find ways to connect with groups you are unfamiliar with.

Virtual Interviews

The year 2020 will be forever remembered as the beginning of the COVID-19 pandemic. COVID-19 changed how we interacted and transformed how many companies do business. One of the biggest adaptations was how virtual meetings became a standard practice in education, business, and at home. Many companies adapted to this change in how they conducted interviews. Rather than in-person interviews, a new staple became *virtual interviews*.

- **Familiarize yourself with the technology.** Since each company you interview with is unique, they will each use a platform they believe suits them best. If you have never used the platform they choose, make sure you take ample time to test out the platform on the laptop or PC you will use for the interview. To make things easier, try to get a partner to conduct this test with – if possible, try to have a partner who is not using the same connection as you. This will ensure that your internet or smart phone's connectivity is tested as well. The last thing you want to worry about is dropped connections or technical issues. Practice a mock interview at the location you will have your interview at.

I also recommend thoroughly testing your connectivity and ensuring you have enough privacy during the entire interview. Make sure you have both sound and picture on your device, and try to test the platform out with someone else.

1. Both you and your partner need to create an account on the platform and install anything that is required.

2. Have your partner serve as the Host of the meeting, since your partner will act as the Interviewer.

3. To avoid feedback from the mic, ensure you are both in separate rooms.

4. Connect to your partner's chat session.

5. Make sure both of you can clearly see and hear each other.

During this test, make note of any technical difficulties

Interview Types

either of you face and how you solved them. If available, test out features like filters and sharing screens if you are going to use them. Familiarize yourself on how to turn these features on and off.

If you can't find another partner to help you test the equipment, but if you have two devices, you can test it out yourself. When I can't find anyone and I need to personally test a new video platform I am unfamiliar with, I will take the following steps:

1. Create two different accounts for the platform. I had one account on my laptop (the device I was planning on using for the interview) and a second account on my smartphone.

2. Ensure both devices are on mute at the beginning to prevent feedback from devices.

3. Host a virtual meeting on one device and invite the other.

4. Once connected, make sure picture quality looks right on both devices. Make sure you are testing in the room you will have the interview in to see if you have proper lighting.

5. Turn on some music in one room and proceed to

move one of the devices outside of the room.

6. Once in the second room, turn on the sound to hear the music from the first room.

7. Test out the other device by playing music in the second room.

8. If available, test out any features like filters and share screen if you are going to use them. Familiarize yourself with how to turn these features on and off.

9. During this test, make note of any technical difficulties you face and how you solved them.

Testing out the platform on two devices accomplishes a second goal: I now have a backup device to use during the interview. I understand you may not be fortunate to have multiple devices available, but it does help prevent potential issues if you have a backup plan in place. At the very least, make sure a phone is handy and you have a point of contact with the employer in case you do have a technical issue before or during the interview.

If you are continuously having problems during your equipment testing, reach out to the company that you will be interviewing with and see if they have any suggestions on how to mitigate these issues. If problems continue to persist, ask if they would be open to using a different platform you are familiar with or if there is a different method to conduct the interview. Ask them about back-up plans on the chance that there could be technical issues. Do not wait until the night before or the day of the test. You want to minimize any unnecessary stress on the day of your interview and at home.

- **Use technology to your advantage.** In one of my first virtual interviews for a position, the company gave me the questions ahead of time. One of the questions was, "Knowing about our current workflow in product development, if there were no restrictions, what changes would you implement?"

Since I had time to prepare, I not only thought of a new process to help improve their workflow, but I also created a small diagram to highlight key points in my response. Instead of holding the diagram up to the camera, I discovered that the video conferencing platform I would use for the interview had a share screen option. After creating my diagram, I tested out the share screen mode and practiced my response.

On the day of my interview, I was well-prepared and presented my response rather than just explaining it to my interviewers. The interviewers were impressed both with my response and for taking the time to actually "present" my response. I was the only one to do so and ended up being one of two people offered a position.

As mentioned before, technology has a tendency to fail. Even though my strategy of sharing screens worked in my favor, I was prepared to present my idea verbally should it fail. The rule of thumb is not to spend too much time troubleshooting if something fails to work. I would say try twice during the interview, and if that doesn't work, find a different way to present your work.

- **Don't look up answers.** In virtual interviews and especially phone interviews, the interviewer cannot see everything an applicant has with them in the room. Because of this, it may be tempting to have a resource to search for the answer to an interview question. Unless otherwise instructed, do not use resources such as books and web pages to look up information. It may backfire. Here are some examples:

    o During the skills assessment portion of a virtual interview, an applicant asked if he could open a tab and look up the answer. We explained that an interview is to assess what he currently knows and not how well he could research the answer.

    o I asked the applicant what he thought of the company's mission and goals. Rather than immediately giving a response, I could hear the applicant typing on a computer and then read the mission statement from the website.

- An applicant kept disconnecting during difficult questions. Even though technical issues can occur during a virtual interview, we realized the applicant was faking the connection issues as a means to stall to find out the answer.

None of the above applicants were hired. Even if you read well, it is hard to disguise that you are reading rather than explaining something in your own words. Your response becomes less personal, and you will lose eye contact with the interviewer. It quickly becomes obvious that your attention is divided.

You also don't want to read from generic sources that may even have incorrect information, as their explanations can sound less conversational. There is a difference between explaining a concept and reciting or reading a definition. An interview is to assess what you currently know, not how well you can search for the answer. It is better to be honest and say you don't know the answer rather than waste the interviewer's time with an answer that is not yours or, even worse, completely incorrect.

Other Recommendations

- Use a stationary chair rather than one that can move

during video interviews, especially if you tend to swivel, rock, or do not realize you are doing so. These movements can become significant distractions, and they may be magnified during the interview.

- Practice Eye Contact. A virtual interview can be tricky to know where to look at times. Position your camera such that you seem to be looking directly at your interviewer.

Phone Interviews

Phone interviews can be tricky since you can't "see" the interviewer(s). The best way to make them easier is by eliminating unnecessary issues that could arise, such as:

- Dropped calls
- Poor audio quality
- Dying/Dead cell phone battery
- Interruptions, Distractions, or Noise

By anticipating issues ahead of time, you can eliminate unnecessary stress and be able to focus solely on the interview itself rather than having to fix issues during the conversation.

Practice

I had the opportunity to work with a new recruiter who did not want to participate in practice phone calls with me. She explained that she is much better at doing it live than role-playing. As I listened to her calls, it was clear she had never practiced talking to applicants before, and she would often steer the conversation off into unrelated tangents, provide irrelevant information, use unprofessional language, or tell bad jokes. Other recruiters soon became irritated by her unprofessional phone calls and urged her to practice before calling more applicants.

It was unfortunate that this recruiter felt she was already very good at speaking on the phone when she clearly had not practiced for this type of call. It wasn't until much intervention and a lot of feedback that she realized she needed to practice more before calling anymore applicants.

Talking on the phone requires practice. How often do you actually call someone on the phone or participate in phone interviews? Calling at least one person a day can help you get used to talking on the phone. If you are preparing for an interview, ask the person on the other end for feedback after the conversation. Asking feedback questions will help you see where you can improve.

- Do I do or say anything that is distracting?
- Are my answers direct, clear, and easy to follow?
- How does the tone of my voice sound?

Cell phone prep: Before your phone interview, there are a few things you should do prior to the interview.

- Know where you are going to take the call. This matters because you want to ensure there will be no distractions or unwanted noise. If you're taking the call at a place of residence, make sure everyone who lives there will respect your privacy and keep noise to a minimum.

- Test your phone where you will hold the interview to identify and avoid dead zones.

- Have a way to ensure your battery does not die mid-call. When I was interviewing for a position at Disney, I had a phone interview with three separate individuals, consecutively, for two hours straight. At the time, I was using a cell phone, and I made sure my phone was plugged into a charger throughout the duration of the interview, so I never had to worry about losing power.

- An alternative to cell phones is using a landline. In my opinion, landlines are best to use for a phone interview since they are not reliant on signal service or a battery. Unlike cell phones, landline calls are less likely to drop the call. If your interviewer uses a cell phone and the call drops, at least it's most likely not your fault. If you are currently at college, some campuses have meeting rooms that you can reserve that have landlines.

Materials: Have reference materials within arms-reach. Your resume is always a good thing to have, since you can refer to experiences that you may have. If you anticipate questions the interviewer may ask, you can have a "cheat sheet" of answers (granted, don't just read from it or you may end up sounding like a robot). It doesn't hurt to also have a bottle of water handy, in case the phone call goes longer than expected and you have been talking for a while. Make sure your materials are organized so you can quickly grab them without scrambling to search for them.

- **Notepad:** You can either type or handwrite notes that come from the phone interview. I personally do the same for in-person interviews, as I want to make notations of answers to questions.

- **Smile:** This may sound odd, but smiling can actually help with your tone. Even though interviewers can't see you, they can "hear" a smile. A friendlier tone of voice is better than an unhappy or monotone one.

Group Interviews

These are my least favorite types of interviews. You are right next to your competition, and you need to show how you are more qualified than the other applicants in the room – all without stepping on the other applicants. The interview may also be perceived as unequal if the interviewer poses different questions to each applicant. However, you never know how many positions are actually available, and you don't want to make others look bad for the sake of a position. Imagine if the employer's intention was to hire everyone in the group if you can cooperate.

- **Short intro:** You will most likely have the opportunity to introduce yourself to the group. Have some talking points ready, such as your background and experience, but keep it short and simple. Have at least one unique thing about yourself to share.

- **Meet and talk to everyone:** Take time to meet everyone. Both the interviewer and the other applicants are all important. You want to be liked by everyone in the room. Even though the others being interviewed might be your competition, you still need to make a good impression. As mentioned earlier, you also don't know how many will actually be offered a position. The employer may also want to see if you can work well in a group environment.

- **Listen To Everyone:** Listen to both the interviewer's and other interviewees responses. The reason you need to listen to everyone's responses is to help you gauge what types of questions are being asked, and what types of responses are being given by the other applicants.

- **Balance answering questions:** When the interviewer poses group questions, strive for a balanced approach.

Take the initiative to answer first at least once. This will show you are not afraid of taking the lead. You do not want to be the last to respond to every question, as this may show you are too timid. Allow others the chance to speak up, and recognize that you don't need to be the center of attention throughout the group interview to be successful.

- **Help others:** Don't be afraid to help others or agree with another applicant's good response. But be genuine about it. I recall a group interview where one applicant mistakenly used terminology from a different company, confusing the interviewer. After a short awkward pause, I chimed in and asked the other applicant a clarifying question that helped him use the correct term for the company. This not only showed I was willing to help another applicant, but it also steered the discussion back on track.

- **Practice:** The key to excelling in a group interview lies in practice interacting in a group. Go to social gatherings where you may not know everyone. Get to know others, and you can practice your introduction, asking questions, and talking/listening in a group setting.

Chapter 9: Presenting Yourself

Focused

The sun was shining, it was a beautiful Saturday morning, and I was eager to meet Sarah, my date, in person for the first time. I didn't have to wait long; soon, a beautiful blonde girl approached me with a smile. I must admit seeing Sarah in person made me even more excited to get to know her. We quickly greeted each other and then entered the restaurant.

Breakfast was simple, and I started to get to know Sarah a bit more by asking her about her family and her interests. One of the questions I asked her was what superpower she'd want if given a choice, and she said teleportation. I also learned that the one place she would love to visit would be Egypt. She also loved roller coasters, and told me a story of how her cell phone partially survived a fall from one.

Conscious of the time, especially since she had plans for the evening, I wanted to ensure our date didn't make her late.

Near the end of the date, I asked her why she was on the dating app that matched us. I asked if she was just looking for friends, casual dating, or perhaps more. She responded, "I have enough friends. I am looking for something serious!"

I excitedly replied that I too was looking for something serious. I then expressed how much I enjoyed our time together and would like to continue to get to know her on another date. She replied that she would love to as well, and confirmed she would be free that Thursday. Our conversation was focused, clear, and purposeful, laying a strong foundation that ultimately led to our marriage.

In a dating situation, your focus should be on your date, the answers to your questions, your body language, etc. Similarly, during an interview, focus on the individual interviewing you. Even though your goal is to get the job offer, you must remember that there is a lot that will happen in a short amount of time during an interview.

- **Pace:** Don't rush into answering a question. Ensure you've understood the question before responding. If you're unclear about what's being asked, don't hesitate to seek clarification. However, be mindful of the time. Most interviewers don't have all the time in the world. Prior to the interview, understand how much time is allotted for the interview and keep your answers on point.

- **Observe:** During the interview, pay keen attention to the interviewer's reactions to your responses, whether verbal or non-verbal. If the interviewer is nodding to a response, oftentimes the interviewer is either subconsciously agreeing to your answer or at least following your explanation. Similarly, if the interviewer looks bored or even looking at a watch, you might be talking too much. As the interview progresses, you want to gather as much information as possible from the interviewer and calibrate your responses accordingly.

- **Remember:** As stated before, the interview serves both the applicant and the interviewer. Try to remember who you meet, their position, and any information they provide about the position or the company. Taking notes during the interview will allow you to remember information that will be beneficial in a few scenarios:

    o **Multiple interviews:** Sometimes a company will have you go through a series of interviews with various levels of management or different departments. If there are multiple interviews, you can refer to individuals by name that you've met along the way or use information that you can refer back to in your responses.

    o **Thank you notes:** This will be covered later in this book, but a short thank you note or email addressed to your interviewer can help you be remembered.

- **First impressions:** If you do end up getting an offer and working for the company, knowing names of individuals and other information can make a good first impression.

- **Determine:** My conversations with Sarah were focused on determining if we were a good match and had the same priorities. Any questions you ask during a job interview should be similarly focused on whether you are a good match for the company and vice versa.

Clear

Before I met my wife, Sarah, I was complaining to a married friend of mine about my dating woes. I explained how I could always get a first date, but it didn't seem that I could ever get a second date. After listening to my sob stories, he then asked a rather introspective question: "Did they know they were on a date?"

At first, I was puzzled—almost offended—he would even suggest that question. Of course, they all knew it was a date! How could they not know? I then started to look at my approach in how I asked these women out. I realized I never once mentioned the word "date" in all my invitations.

After this realization, I started to change my approach and started being a bit more direct, making sure each time I clearly used the word "date." As I made this adjustment, the results led to slightly more rejections, but at least I knew those women were not interested in dating me. I soon realized, however, that the dates I did go on were better quality and there was no question that it was a date and not simply hanging out.

As you interview, you want to be sure you are clear in explaining why you want the job and why you are qualified for the position. To help with clarity, there are some introspective questions that you should ask yourself prior to the interview:

- How can I explain my skills and experiences properly for the position?

- How clear can I be in expressing why I want the position?

- When I practice answering questions, do my body language, responses and tone convey my interest in the position?

- Why am I a better fit than the average applicant?

Throughout the job interview, make sure there is no doubt in the interviewer's mind that you want the job you are applying for. In some circumstances, at the end of the interview, you may want to clearly reiterate that you are interested in the position.

Motivated

What is the main reason I am interested in this position?

We all have different motivations for why we apply for positions. But it's better to be honest about what you want. Once you genuinely understand your intentions and motivations, you can effectively prepare for the interview, articulating both your desire for the role and your qualifications. Such clarity not only helps you but also saves the recruiter time.

If you're targeting a specific company for your career path, you may want to come up with a short explanation about why working for them is important to you during the interview. But a word of caution: simply applying for any position at a company you've always wanted to work with is not always a good idea. This approach can lead to a lack of job satisfaction, as there are no guarantees you can move to your desired position after being hired for the job you applied for.

Compensation is a huge reason for joining a company. However, take time to understand what the company can offer prior to applying. For example, there is a wide difference between what the public sector can offer versus the private sector. As a recruiter, I explain to applicants that if your main motivation is money, the private sector is your best option. I also advise them to think beyond monetary compensation.

For example, if you're looking for job stability/security, insurance, or work opportunities, then take time to find out which companies or organizations can offer these things. Be honest with yourself. You do not have to reveal all your motivations for applying for a position. Having a compelling reason can help motivate you throughout the hiring process.

On the other side, recruiters will be evaluating you against their own criteria. Recruiters are interested in more than just your ability to do a given job; they also want to know your motivation. The reason is because it takes a lot of time and resources to hire a new employee and train a new hire. I want to invest my time and resources in an applicant who will be motivated to work for the company long term. Some questions I think about when evaluating an applicant's motivation are:

- Does the applicant really want the position, or are we a 'fall-back' option?

- Is the applicant actually interested in joining the company?

- Are they aligned with the company's real business, goals, culture, or philosophy?

- If an applicant has an issue with the company itself, are

they likely to seek another position sooner rather than later?

- Is the applicant going to be satisfied with this position?

- If this is a full-time position, is the applicant interested in staying long-term?

For hard to fill positions, the last thing a recruiter wants to do is hire someone who will quit after a short period of time and have to start the search for a replacement all over again. Recruiting, training, and onboarding personnel costs time and resources. Companies want employees who will work long enough for them to see a return on their investment. This is why an applicant's motivation for applying for a position matters to recruiters.

Chapter 10: Strategies for Questions

Answering Questions

A college professor of mine always began his lesson with a story. His stories were so interesting that they always captured everyone's attention. Even though some of his stories were solely for entertainment, most applied to the lesson he was teaching that day.

Throughout the semester, he gave us assignments to write our own stories that were applicable to the principles and concepts taught in class. While this assignment was fun, it made me realize that storytelling is one of the best ways to remember a principle. Even years after taking that class, I still remember the stories he told and their associated lessons.

Who doesn't like a good story? Stories can convey topics and provide a format to guide a listener. Good stories can enhance the retention of information. True stories can inspire. The most impactful stories impart lessons that we can learn from and implement in our lives. Through such stories, we foster experiences that shape us into the people we want to be.

A large part of answering interview questions is talking about your experiences. Telling stories of your experiences helps people remember you. Equally important, it makes it easy for you to remember your own experiences as you practice retelling them. Share them with everyone, be it with people you meet during your daily commute to work or people you meet at school. Practice makes perfect.

If you have trouble telling your stories, try writing them out first. Writing out your experiences can help you remember details that are important and see how you can make your story flow better. Capture as much detail as possible at the start. Then pare it down to what is important and practice telling it to someone. To find out what details are key to your stories, listen to what questions others ask you when you retell your experience.

Make sure you are clear and concise when telling your stories during an interview. I recommend thinking of a short 30 second to one minute version and then a longer three-minute version if you can. Once you practice both the short and long versions, you can make adjustments when you are speaking to the interviewer.

Most interviewers will only want the short version due to time constraints. However, if you see the interviewer has an interest in what you are saying, you can expound on a point or two. The part you want to add the most detail to is the action you took. If the interviewer wants more details, then you can pull in details from your longer version to extend the explanation.

- Answer the question as directly, clearly, and concisely as possible. You only have a limited amount of time during an interview. Because of this, you don't want to give a long explanation if the question is asking for a simple "yes" or "no" response. Use stories when it's appropriate.

- Show your interest in the position through your tone, energy, and body language.

- Don't use slang or profanity when answering questions. Refrain from using language that is unprofessional in any manner.

- Practice answering questions. The more you practice, the easier it will be to convey your responses.

The Power of Three

During an interview, you'll likely be asked open-ended questions, including the popular, "tell me about yourself." Usually, you don't have a lot of time to respond, and your answer could easily veer off track: You may go too deep into your personal history, or talk about topics that might not be relevant to the interview. Think about what the interviewer truly wants to know.

This is where the "Power of Three" strategy comes into play. When preparing a speech or answering a question that has numerous possible answers, pick three subtopics you can talk about. Organizing your thoughts in this manner will help you streamline your answer.

Using three subtopics will also help guide your audience throughout your response. If you go beyond three subtopics, it becomes increasingly difficult for both you and someone else to recall what you talked about. Organize your response as follows:

- **Statement:** Begin by outlining how you'll address the question with three relevant subtopics. This should be one sentence, introducing the three points you'll expand upon. This sets the stage for the rest of your response.

- **Transition words**: Each subtopic should begin with a transition word. A simple way is to literally state "First," "Second," and "Last." These transition words will act as a guide to the listener throughout your response. The final point should be introduced with a conclusive transition like "Finally" to signal the end of the final subtopic you want to talk about.

- **Re-state**: Finish by summarizing the three main points you've presented in response to the question.

For the "tell me about yourself" question, think of it as a verbal cover letter. Pick three relevant subtopics that answer why you applied for the job. Here is one example:

- **Education and skills**: Highlight the skills and knowledge you have acquired that qualify you for the position.

- **Related Experience**: Talk about relevant experience that can translate into potential success for the position. Focus on the impact of your contributions.

- **Professional Goals**: Discuss how this job fits into your professional goals and why you want the job.

I would suggest playing to your strengths and thinking about what three things you can highlight about yourself that qualify you for the position you are applying for. After you have an outline, you can start filling in the details to craft a response.

PAR: Problem Action Resolution

In an interview, your goal is to get the job, and this means providing strong responses to interview questions. To accomplish this, you should aim for PAR. No, I am not talking about your golf score. In this case, PAR stands for Problem, Action, and Resolution. Questions can be difficult if you're not prepared. However, breaking up your answer into these three distinct parts makes answering these types of questions much easier.

- **Problem: What was the issue, challenge, or situation?** Brief explanation of what happened. You don't need to give all the details, but offer enough so the interviewer grasps the context.

- **Action: What did you do?** This forms the crux of your storytelling that showcases your skills. Do not talk about what other people did unless it's pivotal to highlighting your role. The interviewer wants to know what you did.

- **Resolution: What was the outcome of your actions?** This is the conclusion of your story. The main idea of this is to explain the outcome or impact of your actions.

Let's look at an example:

Question: Have you ever worked with a person who was less capable and what did you do about it?

- **Problem:** When I was in college in the information systems program, I was assigned a group where one member never learned how to properly code and struggled with technical concepts.

- **Action:** While it was frustrating having a technically weak teammate in a project that required technical/development skills, I wanted to make the most of his strengths. I learned he was very good at public speaking. Because of this, I made sure he was the lead speaker in our presentations. As a side benefit of helping him prepare, I taught him technical concepts that he lacked.

- **Resolution:** The result was that we were able to gain top marks on our capstone project for both the program we developed and our presentation.

Sometimes the results of your quantifiable accomplishments are more impressive than the steps you took to get there. In order to ensure you have the interviewer's attention, you should lead with the results or impact of your actions.

PAR: Problem Action Resolution

For example, if you increased revenue by 50%—or even better, have an actual dollar amount—you may want to bring these facts up earlier in your response. After you get used to telling stories using the PAR method, consider opening with a result-driven statement to underscore your accomplishments, thereby capturing the interviewer's attention, before describing the situation and the action you took.

Sample Interview Questions

Have you ever failed at something?

Through this question, the interviewer is really trying to find out what you did after the failure, rather than the failure itself. No one is perfect, and the interviewer already understands this. What they want to know is: What did you do to either fix the issue or improve the situation? How are you currently trying to work/overcome/improve from that setback? What did you learn from this experience?

This also gives you the chance to show that you are willing to own up to your mistakes rather than blame someone else for the failed results. Showing that you have made mistakes is not only human, but also displays the attribute of humility. Everyone eventually fails at something, whether it's missing a deadline or a poor project outcome. Failure is part of life.

Tell me about a time when you worked with a difficult person.

For this situational question, use a PAR story. In any job you take, you may not always have the opportunity to work with people you get along with. Eventually, you will work with someone who doesn't agree with you or get along with you. Do not mention names, as they are irrelevant details. Also, the world is small; the person interviewing you might know the person, and you never want to put anyone in a bad light or draw attention to another person in your interview. The main point here is to see if you are able to work past issues with others and get the job done.

- **Problem:** One time I worked in a group with a co-worker who was not very good at working on group projects that required a lot of technical aspects, but she would be more than happy to claim credit for the work that was done. None of my co-workers liked working with her.

- **Action:** I knew I would one day have to work with her on a project and took time to find out her strengths and interests. After some time, I found that she was good at making graphics and diagrams.

- **Resolution:** In the end, when I was paired up with her, I made sure there was some part of the project that required either graphics or diagrams and explained to her that I believed she could do a far better job than I ever could. It took time, and it wasn't always easy, but I believe giving her confidence and a role to fill allowed us to work together on projects.

Please describe your background and/or experience in the fields of (insert related field of study for the position).

Here you need to create an organized and brief elevator pitch about yourself relating to the field of study. This is an excellent case for using the power of three. Here are some suggestions:

- **Education:** Start with your formal education if it relates to the position. If you do not have a relevant degree, you can mention any relevant training or certifications you have completed.

- **Previous Positions and Experience:** Briefly explain the most relevant work experiences you have had. For example, you can summarize and talk about highlights of your career experience.

- **Keeping Current:** Talk about how you keep your skills sharp. What kind of new training are you taking? What kinds of personal projects are you working on? How do you keep abreast of the current trends in the industry?

How are you continuing your education or developing relevant skills?

Training courses or certifications that directly relate to the position and the estimated date of completion should be mentioned. If you are not taking any formal education, you can mention what you are reading on a daily basis to keep up with the latest trends in the industry.

Personal projects or things you do as a hobby that develop or use skills the job requires might be worth mentioning. Anything you bring up at this point should be related to the job's requirements.

What is your greatest weakness?

During an interview, one applicant started talking about how he is a perfectionist and makes sure his projects are always top quality. I told the applicant that what he was talking about wasn't an actual weakness.

Everyone has weaknesses. For this question, keep it short and to the point, but know that you must mention an actual weakness. Naming something that is an actual strength, like working too hard, does not answer the question. Recruiters are wise to this trick and it will not help you.

The main point is to show that you are self-aware of at least one thing you can improve upon and, more importantly, how you are working on it. Try to pick something that is not an essential skill for the job.

End on a positive note of how you are working on it. Talk about methods you have discovered to help you overcome that weakness, or how you're actively working to improve it.

What was the most challenging experience you have faced?

This is another great example of a PAR question. Start answering this question with a brief explanation of the problem. Your focus should be on what you did to overcome the challenge. Make sure you clearly explain the steps and actions you took to overcome the challenge. Remember to end with an explanation of the results or impact of your actions.

What would you do if your supervisor gave you five projects to complete in a certain amount of time but you knew you could only finish four?

This is not only a hypothetical question where you can be creative, but it can also be a bit tricky as you can head down several avenues when answering this question. You don't want to ramble. Aim for a structured response. Use the power of three to narrow down your answer. For example, focus on these three categories: prioritization, communication, and delegation.

- **Prioritization:** Since you can only finish four in the

given time frame, you will need to explain how you would rank projects.

- **Communication:** Explain how you would talk to your supervisor, stakeholders, and teammates about work expectations.

- **Delegation:** Since the fifth project is considered impossible to finish on your own, to whom would you reach out for help?

How have you demonstrated leadership in the workplace?

Leadership can be found in many ways. The obvious answer lies in leading a team or project. However, even within your designated role, leadership opportunities arise. For example, if you learn something new that is useful for others in the workplace, you could teach others what you have learned. Mentoring or teaching others is also a huge leadership role that doesn't require a direct title or assignment.

Tell me about a time when you were asked to do something out of your comfort zone.

We have all done something that stretches us. If possible, try to choose a skill or a task that is relevant to the job you are applying for. Then explain what you did to adapt to the situation and what you learned to help you the next time you face a similar situation.

What do you do when faced with a difficult choice?

This is another question where you want to anchor your response around a specific event. Since this can go a number of ways, it's best to pick one experience and use that as an example to convey your reasoning behind your decision-making process. Whether you weighed pros and cons or sought advice, ensure your methodology is simple and easy to follow. Employ the PAR method if necessary.

Have you ever had a job or task that you felt was boring? What did you do?

These can be anything. It can refer to routine or seemingly mindless tasks that you are given. A lot of temporary jobs have tasks that, while important, can cause boredom overtime. Regardless of how you answer this question, you want to ensure you display a positive attribute that reflects well on you. Here are some examples of attributes:

- **Perspective:** Looking at the task from a different perspective made it more meaningful.

    Example: A large part of business analytics is looking at large amounts of data. Sometimes, this data is "dirty" and needs cleaning and formatting before analysis.

While this is not the most enjoyable aspect of the job, it is a vital part of the process.

- **Gamification:** Turning tasks into games can increase productivity or improve morale. Can implement incentives or prizes.

Example: One of my first jobs was working with my brother in a warehouse for an electrical construction company. One of my tasks was preparing prefabrication boxes for drywall construction. Each box required certain holes to be punched, connectors attached, and a ground wire fastened to the center. This was a very tedious and manual process. To make the job 'fun', my brother and I would create games and races to see how fast we could complete a batch of prefabrication boxes.

- **Innovation:** Finding a better way to do something or improving the processes.

Example: Often, routine manual processes can be automated. This is especially true with technology. When I was a consultant for the healthcare industry, I was tasked with consolidating large datasets of hospital data for a dashboard that would essentially produce a daily scorecard for each hospital. When I saw how the data was being handled and processed manually, I saw an opportunity: writing a script that would do everything that was needed to consolidate the data.

Why Do You Want to Work for Us?

Believe it or not, the reason for applying for a position can be a very telling question for the interviewer. I have conducted many interviews where the applicant could not articulate the reason why they applied to work for the company other than the job that met their skill set. The applicant did not know the company's real business, goals, culture, or philosophy.

When applying for any job, researching the company is just as important. Even if the position itself is a fit for you, ensure you take some time to familiarize yourself with the company's goals and how your desired role feeds into that vision.

If your values don't align with the company's, you may face challenges in the position despite having all the qualifications for the job itself. Remember this: where you work is just as important, if not more important, than what you end up doing for the company.

Questions you may want to find the answers to when applying to a company:

- Do I believe in this company's mission and goals?

- Do I understand the position and how it fits into the

company's operations?

- Do I meet all or most of the qualifications for the position I am applying for? If not, how do I plan to bridge those gaps, or what other skills or experiences can I leverage?

- Is this the only role in the company I'm interested in?

- Do I see myself being able to pivot to other positions in this company if my position becomes obsolete?

- What does my future look like at this company?

- Would I be a good fit for this company?

- If I was hired, what would I have to offer?

- Are there any conditions or constraints associated with working here, and do I understand them all?

- Will the position demand relocation, and are my loved ones supportive of such a move?

These questions are meant to get you started if you're not sure where to begin. Come up with your own questions and start finding out the answers to them. While you may not be able to find out all the answers, the more you are able to find out on your own can help you make a well-informed decision and prepare you for the interview.

Chapter 11: Answering and Asking Questions

Occupation Specific Questions

For any job that requires a special skill set, you will most likely be asked questions to test your knowledge in that occupation. The only way to do well with these questions is to make sure you are up-to-date with knowledge, skills, and abilities in your respective field. To improve your preparation for these questions, find ways to develop your expertise in the field.

How to Prepare

- **Practice:** Regardless of how experienced you are in your field, consider taking classes or earning relevant certifications to keep your skills current and sharp. When I see a resume from a student or a recent graduate lacking a relevant degree for a position, more often than not, I don't proceed further. The exception is if the individual has directly relevant work experience in the field. However, if you don't have the educational background and are called for an interview, be prepared for questions assessing your knowledge of the job.

- **Keep current:** Staying up-to-date with current events helps you understand industry trends within your field. This can also guide you towards areas you need to study or skills you must acquire. Familiarize yourself with companies in your occupational field. See what these companies are investing in, what customers they interact with, or what direction they are looking to go in.

During a pre-screen phone call with an applicant for a software development position, I asked the applicant how she keeps up with technology. She explained how challenging it was to keep up with all the changes in the industry and expressed how her current role and personal life keep her too busy to carve out time for anything else. Even though I appreciated her honesty, her response showed a lack of desire to prepare for change.

Possible Types of Questions

- **Definitional:** Some skills assessments solely evaluate your ability to define common terms or concepts. This is the most basic type of assessment, as it doesn't go beyond testing your ability to memorize. However, there is one issue with these kinds of questions or assessments, namely that they don't effectively test your understanding of the material.

- **Give an example:** When I ask a skills question, I usually follow it with "Can you give me an example?" This approach is to test if the applicant can think of a way to explain the concept beyond a mere definition. With more experienced applicants, I sometimes rephrase this by adding, "If you were tasked with teaching this concept to an intern or in a mentoring role, how would you explain this concept?"

- This can also help me assess if an applicant is able to adjust their explanations to different levels of understanding. There will be opportunities where you will need to explain a complex topic to someone who lacks expertise in your field. To really test your knowledge of your field, see if there are ways you can explain to both a novice and expert in your field.

Occupation Specific Questions

- **Application questions:** These types of questions test your ability to apply a concept or think in terms of using your skills to handle a scenario. For example, as a recruiter, I would rephrase skills-based questions to look like: "In what situation would you employ (occupation specific term)?"

When I was hiring for business analytics, I would sometimes want a more holistic view of their thought process and would give them a specific scenario, such as forecasting demand for a product. I would then want the applicant to walk me through their approach.

To clarify, I would explain that I would want to know the answers to the questions, such as what kind of data they would want to look at, what kind of techniques they would employ to analyze the data, or what tools they would use. Depending on their response, I may delve deeper and ask the question, "Why?"

- **Project sample:** While this isn't a type of question, projects can give a perspective on your ability in that respective occupation. On a daily basis, I receive a lot of applicants who are still working on their academics and have very limited relevant work experience. If given the opportunity, I ask them what they are currently working on outside of school projects. Are they working on something that is not assigned to them? Are they learning something new or going beyond what was assigned to them? Working on self-initiated projects can keep your skills sharp and increase your abilities. Sometimes they may be more impressive than a school assigned project.

Make sure it is a project you did and you are prepared to explain everything about it. I have been in interviews where the applicant wasn't even able to explain what they did or answer basic questions regarding the project. In one instance, the applicant wasn't even able to tell me what programming language the application was written in!

During an interview, one applicant shared a personal project. Throughout the demo and explanation of the project, he managed to pre-emptively answer knowledge-based questions I was going to ask him later on in the interview.

Ultimately, this showed he not only knew how to explain the concepts, but he also demonstrated his ability to apply them correctly as well. Since there was no need to ask him those questions, I could evaluate him for a more senior level position than what he initially applied for and ask more advanced questions.

In the end, I was able to offer a more advanced position

with a better salary that could use his level of abilities.

If you are a mid-careerist, it might be worthwhile to have some type of personal project to provide during an interview if all your work projects are sensitive or proprietary in nature. During an interview with an applicant who claimed 10 years of relevant work experience, he was not able to articulate his projects well enough for us to evaluate his abilities. Everything was explained in general terms, and we felt that we were unable to make a clear determination of what he had actually accomplished.

If you are in a position where you have signed a Non-Disclosure Agreement (NDA) or your work is classified, either have a personal project that can demonstrate your abilities or practice a way to explain your projects in an unclassified, non-sensitive manner.

Logic Questions

These can either be fun or annoying, depending on your point of view. The main purpose of these questions is to gauge your thought process. Some of these questions may not even have a real answer.

Unfortunately, there's no foolproof method for teaching logic. The only way to perhaps prepare for these types of questions is to practice giving instructions. For example, if you like to bake, see if you can describe the process of doing that requires a series of steps, like baking a cake.

Try to explain each part so that someone can follow your instructions. In addition to explaining each step, understand 'why' each step is taken. The point is to practice talking through the way you would approach a certain problem, which is often more important to the interviewer than the answer itself.

Once, during an interview with a company, I was presented with a 30-question logic test within a 30-minute time frame. Post-assessment, the interviewer gave me verbal problem-solving questions:

Pick a Matching Pair: You enter a dark room and find a

drawer that has 10 black socks and 10 white socks. How many do you need to pick until you have a matching pair?

Fix the Signs: You are at the market, and there are three baskets of fruit. They are all labeled incorrectly. One says apples, another says oranges, and the last is mixed (apples and oranges). If you cannot look in the baskets and have to reach into just one basket, which one would you choose in order to fix the signs?

After each of my responses, he asked, "Why?" While I did get the correct answers for both questions, he was more focused on the logical explanation behind my responses than the answer being correct.

Years have since passed, and in my role as a recruiter, I often used similar logic questions in my interviews, especially with potential interns. However, once the interviewee arrives at an answer, I usually ask one additional follow-up question:

- Hypothetically speaking, if lives were at stake and the answer to this problem meant success or failure, how confident are you in your answer?

When other recruiters hear this follow-up question, they think that I'm pretty brutal. I then explain my reasoning. If I am looking for the best person for a position, I want to evaluate the individual beyond normal circumstances. While this is not a perfect tactic, I can gain more information than just the right or wrong answer.

- How confident is the applicant in their original answer?
- Does the applicant back down from a correct answer when challenged?
- How does the applicant deal with a stressful situation?
- What does the applicant do when there are high stakes involved?

You might be wondering what the answers are regarding the logic questions I mentioned earlier. Fear not, here they are:

- **Pick a Matching Pair** – The correct answer is three socks. The reason is that the first two socks you choose will give you one of three pairs: two black, two white, or one black and one white. You have a one-third chance that it will not be a matching pair. After picking a third sock, you have at least one matching pair.

- **Fix the Signs** – The correct answer is choosing from the mixed basket. Since all the signs are incorrect, you know this basket cannot be mixed but must either be the all apple or all orange basket. Once you've drawn from it, you know with 100% certainty which basket you have. Once you know this basket, the others can be figured out through the process of elimination. For example, if you draw an apple from the mixed basket, then you know it is the apple basket and the other two must be the orange or mixed. Since one is labeled orange, and all the signs are incorrect, this one must be the mixed basket and the other must be the orange basket. This one is easier to understand if you draw out a chart.

	Apples	**Oranges**	**Mixed**
Possible Outcomes	Oranges only or Mixed	Apples only or Mixed	Apples only or Oranges only
Logic	50% chance it's an Apple - if so, then this is the mixed basket.	50% chance it's an Orange - if so, then this is the mixed basket.	100% certainty that it's either a basket of Apples only or Oranges only.

Trap Questions

There are what I term 'Trap Questions' in interviews. Sometimes interviewers are tricky and want to find out if you are worth investing in. It takes time and money to hire a new employee for a company, and employers want to find the best applicant for the job. To thin out the number of applicants, they may ask what I call "trap questions" in order to find out certain information, such as your motivations for applying.

These filter questions can help the employer learn more about your actual intentions and motivations for applying for the job. The motivational factor for each applicant can vary, so the interviewer may ask questions to find out what they need most from a new employee. For example, if a company needs someone long-term, they may think of questions that touch on loyalty to the company.

Do you have any other job offers?

Depending on how competitive you are as an applicant, this may work in your favor as it may push the recruiter to make a larger effort to get someone that is sought after. However, I usually err on the side of caution and choose not to reveal too much about the offer if I do have one. I will stress that verbal offers do not count.

Which office location are you applying for?

This question usually only comes up for large firms that have multiple offices either across the nation or even world-wide. Even though the company may say they are looking to fill positions all over, this is only half true. The recruiter actually knows the number of positions in the area they are covering.

For example, if you are at a job fair in San Jose, California, most likely the recruiter is from that area and knows the positions that need to be filled. They may advertise all locations throughout the nation, but they will only have very basic information regarding these other locations. So, if you inform a San Jose recruiter that you're looking to apply for a role in Florida, anticipate an additional layer to your interview process, as your application would be referred to the recruiter overseeing the Florida region.

How much do you want to get paid?

As a recruiter, if I don't already have this information, the first question I'll pose to a potential applicant concerns their salary expectations. I ask this initially because I already know the hiring requirements, including the salary range for each position. Because I don't want to waste my time with an individual who may have an unrealistic salary requirement,

I'd rather know this information upfront.

On the other hand, this is my least favorite question to answer as an applicant. The reason is that if you answer too high, you won't be offered the job. Pitch too low, and that's the offer you might receive. So, where does the balance lie?

For starters, begin by researching the industry average of what that position currently pays for. If you have contacts within the company you are applying to, you may be able to get a feel or understand how much they typically pay for that position. Importantly, nothing surpasses the value of relevant work experience, which often serves as a marker for performance. If you bring experience to the table, you can lean towards the higher end of the range, especially with many years under your belt.

Recognized certifications and education can also help move you up on the scale, but they can only go so far if you have no relevant work experience in the field. As long as you can logically walk the recruiter through the reasons you should get that particular salary, the recruiter may consider your number. A clever approach, but difficult to achieve, is somehow getting the recruiter to reveal this information before you share your expectations.

One thing to note, though, is that money isn't everything. Remember that the initial offer is not where you stay if the company promotes regularly, gives bonuses, or may have other benefits that may outweigh the money.

Why did you leave your last position?

This is a question where you will need to be honest, but there's no need to delve into every detail. If prospective employers contact your previous ones for references, they might seek their perspective, especially if they have concerns.

If you left on negative terms, you do not need to go into the details or focus on the negative side of things. Rather, be brief on the reason you left and focus on positive aspects such as lessons learned, what excites you about the position, or how your past experiences qualify you for the position.

Would you rather have more time off or more money?

This all depends on your needs. Be honest with yourself and what you truly value. Also, take into account what type of company you are applying to. Do their employees expect to work long hours? If so, they may lean towards monetary compensation over time off. Again, every company is different. Do your research and plan accordingly for your responses to what you are looking for in terms of compensation.

Have you ever had to work under a manager who was difficult or unrealistic?

This question might bring out negative emotions. The trick is to not focus on the manager but rather on how you dealt with the difficult situation. Try not to name names or reveal gender to avoid triggering an interviewer's unconscious biases. Briefly explain the situation, but focus more on what you did or learned from the experience and how you would do things differently.

Is this the only position you are interested in?

At times, recruiters might question your commitment and resolve to the position you've applied for. The recruiter may not feel completely confident in your ability to do the job you are applying for or may believe your experience fits better in another position at their company.

Remember, you are being interviewed for a specific position at the moment. There is a risk of entertaining a different position that might not be available, especially if it isn't immediately available. Counter this question by reiterating why you are interested in the position you are currently being interviewed for and how you qualify.

Illegal Questions

Some questions are actually illegal to ask. These questions fall under the protected classes/attributes for equal employment and to prevent employment discrimination.

- Protected classes/attributes include: age, race, color, religion, sex/gender, marital status, national origin, genetic information, and disability.

Larger companies are usually aware of these categories due to their fear of lawsuits. They have strong Legal and Human Resource departments to help them navigate interviews properly and eliminate the use of illegal questions. However, start-ups or smaller, family-owned businesses might not exhibit the same level of caution.

Another case is when some interviewers are not properly trained to conduct a fair and equitable interview. The interviewer might actually be an employee who is either a supervisor or a team member and was asked to vet your skills for the job. If this is the case, they may have had little to no training in what they should or shouldn't ask during an interview. They may also have yet to receive training on how to mitigate their own bias. When this happens, interviewers might not actually mean to ask illegal questions.

In any case, the best approach is often to address the underlying concern that prompted the question. The following are some of these illegal questions that hopefully you will never encounter. Each question is followed by a response that you can give.

What is your marital status?

These personal questions have nothing to do with your capability or ability to do the job. One way to answer this is: "My personal life will not interfere or prevent me from doing this job."

Do you have any disabilities?

As long as you are physically and mentally able to perform the job, having a disability should not be held against you. If you are asked this question, you can reply, "I am able to do this job." Prior to the interview, ask if there are any reasonable accommodations that they provide, should you require them.

As stated before, do not let your disability define you. I had an applicant who had a disability but seemed qualified to do the job. However, throughout the entire hiring process, he would repeatedly bring up his disability. Even before I could explain how the interview worked, he immediately asked for "unlimited time" as a "reasonable accommodation". I explained that it would not be possible since those conducting the interview did not have an infinite amount of time to give one applicant. This was not a reasonable request.

How old are you?

As long as you are of the legal age for the profession, age should never bar you from a position. You can kindly respond, "I meet the age requirement for this position."

What is your religious affiliation or holidays you observe?

This question might be asked because the interviewer wants to know if your religion will prevent you from working on certain days. You can respond, "I am able to work the required hours of operation."

Are you a US citizen?

This question might be illegal, depending on the organization or employer you're applying to. For positions with the US federal government or ones that require a security clearance, it is not illegal to inquire an applicant's US citizenship status. This will require a direct 'yes' or 'no' response. Often, it is rephrased as a statement or qualification, such as "this position requires US citizenship. Do you meet this requirement?"

For non-federal government positions or if citizenship is not a direct requirement, you may answer that you are legally able to work in the US as your response. If you are not a citizen, make sure to verify whether it is a requirement before applying.

Interviewing for Internal Positions

Sometimes the position you are looking for may be within the company you already work for. The rules and resources slightly differ when it comes to internal job interviews. For example, you might be able to visit the office or department before you apply for the position. One thing is certain, learn about how your company operates, understand the politics, and leverage your network.

Use your relationships and network within the company to your advantage. Since you are currently working at this company, see if you can find out who you might be working with in this new position. Learn who you would report to and who has worked under this individual. If you don't know who these people are or if the position is in another department that you've never worked with, you need to do some research prior to the interview.

Reach out to others in that department, gain a sense of who works there, ask for their opinions, and get a clearer picture of what you'll actually be doing. This will also help you build a better case for why you want the job. Some other things to keep in mind when applying for an internal position are:

- **The position may have been posted with an individual already in mind.** Some companies are required to exhibit equitable opportunities and must post a position that is available to all employees before it can be filled. However, sometimes a position might open up with a preferred applicant in mind. Even though these politics may be in place, it is worth putting forth your best effort during the process, because that office might have other opportunities for you or create one for you.

- **Only apply if you genuinely want the position.** As a current employee of the company, you don't want to burn any bridges. This includes wasting others' time. Remember, it takes time to review an application, set up an interview, conduct an interview, and make a decision.

- **Do your research.** Find out all you can about not only the position itself but other important details, such as:

    o **Supervisor** – A supervisor can make or break the position. Even if the position is your dream position, a poor supervisor can often make the position undesirable.

    o **Coworkers** – Similar reasons as a supervisor. Understand the team dynamics. Try to find out how helpful they are and what they like or don't like about working in this department or office. Learn as much as you can about the office culture.

- **Customers** – Understanding who the customer is will help you prepare your answers for the interview. Learn about the types of deliverables, communication styles, and expectations. If you already understand the customer or have worked with a similar one, you'll be able to instil confidence in the interviewer regarding your ability to ensure customer satisfaction.

- **Challenges** – Find out how to prepare for known challenges or issues individuals face in the position. Understand past mistakes that others have made, and prepare for them.

- **Key Skills/Experience** – Identify the core day-to-day skills required for the position and think of relevant experiences to prove you are qualified for the position.

* **Always Try Your Best.** In certain circumstances, you may be interviewed by someone you already know. Perhaps you have previously worked with the individual or there's some other connection where the interviewer knows you personally. Whatever the reason is, if you really want the job, do not fall under the

assumption that the job is already yours. Even if the interviewer is familiar with you, you must still give your best effort.

While the interview might appear to be a mere formality, remember that as long as there are other applicants, the job is not yet yours. A personal connection may provide you with an advantage over other applicants, but it should not be the only reason you are offered a position in the end. There's always the possibility that someone else might outperform you in the interview and get the position.

Rather than relying entirely on your reputation or your network, prove that you are the most qualified for the position. Other than preparing for the interview itself, one strategy is to bring a solution or innovative idea to the interview. Your previous research on the position will help generate ideas.

Sample Questions

What are your career goals and how would this position serve to advance those goals?

Try to plan at least a position or two beyond the one you are currently in. Always have a goal. Answering this question by logically explaining where you want to be and how the position can help you gain the necessary skills or experience is a good way to answer this question.

In one experience, prior to applying for a position, a manager in the group asked me how taking the position would help me in my career. It was a good introspective question as to why I wanted the position. My answer also gave the manager insight into my motivations for applying and how he could best help me in my career.

What aspect of this position interests you the most and why?

Ensure you've thoroughly researched the position. Visit the office prior to applying. Try to find out as much as you can beforehand. Learn about the projects the office is currently working on or their future plans. Perhaps you found out the types of challenges the office is facing. Any of these reasons are good to show you want to contribute to the office's success in achieving its goals.

What new ideas would you implement if you were in the position?

Prior to applying, visit the office and try to find out what pain points they have or how they operate on a day-to-day basis. Think of a solution to any issues or innovate a better way to do something. If you come up with an idea, one way to stand out during the interview is to create a handout that contains a basic outline of the idea.

Remember, this should be an idea that you are willing to give up freely. There is a chance the office will like the idea but not offer you the position in the end. Keep it simple and use the power of three. Choose three steps or parts that explore the idea, but do not go into all the details. Stay high-level. If you use handouts of any sort, you must walk the interviewer(s) through them.

Tell us a time when you worked under a difficult manager or with a problematic colleague.

As mentioned earlier, refrain from using any names, pronouns, or exact timelines, as these can generate bias. No matter how large a company is, you never know who knows who. Ensure you end with either a positive resolution or lessons learned.

How did you prepare for this interview?

The point of this question is to find out who you talked to regarding the position, what you found out, and what other actions you took based on your research. You can back up your claims by mentioning individuals in the group you spoke to during your preparation or perhaps any training you are taking to prepare for the position. This would be one of the exceptions to which you may mention names.

Asking Questions

Almost every interview will end with, "Do you have any questions?" If you don't have any questions, it may show that you have not prepared adequately enough or are not truly interested in the position. This is your chance to find out more information or clarify anything you are unsure of.

Sometimes, asking questions can actually make or break the interviewer's final opinion of you. Throughout the interview, there are a few moments for you to truly differentiate yourself. A good question can help those interviewing you remember you and set you apart from all the other dull or forgettable applicants.

When I interviewed with an accounting firm for an internship, there were multiple stages. There must have been at least 40 applicants who were all interviewing for a position. One of the parts the associates all stressed was the large group panel Q&A with five of the senior partners of the accounting firm. They told everyone several times to think of good questions to ask the partners.

On the day of the partner panel, many applicants began by asking questions regarding the firm's future state and how the economy might affect the nature of their business. I was honestly bored by all of these questions. They did not answer what I actually wanted to know. I wanted to know more about how I could contribute to the company if I were to be hired. Also, by reading the room, the partners, while respectful to the questions asked, didn't seem excited about the questions either. I then posed the question:

"As senior partners, what do you feel is the greatest challenge a new hire would typically face within the first few weeks, and how would you recommend overcoming or preparing for it?"

After asking that question, all five senior partners took time to answer the question. I also overheard a few associates whisper, "Who asked that question?" and "What is his name?" There are a few interesting parts to this question. First, it asks for direct advice from the interviewer (in this case, directly to the partners). Secondly, it tells the interviewer that you are genuinely interested in getting the position to the point that you want to be a contributor from day one. This question never ceases to impress the interviewer. These are the kinds of moments you want to have during an interview.

Think of questions you genuinely want answers to. Remember, you don't want to ask questions you can find the answers to on your own. Do your research. Look up information about the company. For starters, look at the website. Find out as much as you can, e.g., the mission of the company, customers, partners, compensation, benefits, etc. Start making a list of questions about what is important to you, and find as many answers as you can. The more information you find, the clearer your decision about working in that position will be. Once you have done your due diligence, you should have a better set of questions to ask during the interview.

The interviewer's objective may be to determine if you should be offered the position, but your objective is to see if you actually want to take it. There is no perfect job or company. There will always be positives and negatives. Find out what they are.

Suggestions:

- What do you like most about working for this company, and how long have you been here?

- What do you like the least about working for this company?

- What is the work culture here like?

- What are the difficult decisions I will have to make in this position?

- What accomplishments are expected of a new hire in the first six months of their first year?

- What differentiates good employees from great employees?

- What are your expectations for someone in this position?

- What are the most important skills for this position?

- What qualities are most valued at this company?

- What opportunities for growth are there in this position?

- What are the big challenges you have with your customers/stakeholders?

- What are the next steps after this interview?

- When will a decision be made?

Leave out questions that the interviewer will most likely not have the answers to or questions that they will most likely not answer. For example, questions that don't have anything to do with the position itself and are more suitable for human resources (such as compensation or benefits) are best kept until you have already been offered the position and need to make a decision if you want to accept the job or not.

Save compensation or benefit questions until after you receive an offer or at a time when you can negotiate. More often than not, the ones interviewing you may not know the answers to these types of questions. Bringing up questions regarding compensation and benefits too early in the interview process, especially in a first-round interview, may lead the interviewer to believe your motivations are one-sided.

Questions to Ask During Internal Interviews

Earlier, I explained the concept of applying for internal positions within a company where you're currently employed. Interviewing for an internal position also requires a fair bit of research. However, you might have additional resources, such as the ability to visit the office prior to the interview and speak with individuals on that team.

Once, I saw an internal posting for an applications developer position that seemed like a good fit for me. The project I would be working on sounded interesting, and I believed that taking the position would be a good career move. I reached out to the point of contact for the position and asked to schedule an office visit.

During the office visit, I met with the lead software developer of the team I'd potentially be joining — essentially, my prospective supervisor. I also had the opportunity to speak with others on that team. Some of the questions I asked were:

How large is the group I would be working in, and what is the culture like?

Those with whom you work are probably the most important

factor when moving to another position. Regardless of how interesting or engaging the work is, if you can't get along with your coworkers, it might not be worth pursuing.

What are the core work hours?

It's always important to know when you're expected to be at work. Some offices have a set schedule for meetings that require your attendance or when your customers are more available. Find out when you are expected to be at work in order to avoid building a reputation for tardiness or absence.

What are your daily, weekly, and monthly expectations of your team?

Understand what your deliverables and objectives are to ensure success. By asking this question, you can gain a sense of how much pressure the job entails in regards to deadlines and how you can best prepare for them.

How long have you worked in this position?

Anyone who will rate/review your performance can make or break a position. I have worked with my fair share of good and poor supervisors. The best supervisors I have worked with were also good mentors and helped me grow in my career. The reason you want to know how long a supervisor has served in the position is to see how much experience they have in that role. This is also a good question to ask any of your potential coworkers.

How long do you expect to stay with this group?

Along similar lines, finding out the supervisor's experience in a management role is to see if they are deciding to move to another position or not. I previously took a position partially because I really wanted to work with a supervisor who had a stellar reputation. However, unknown to me, he was in the process of moving to another position a month after I started.

What is the biggest struggle this group has?

Finding out the pain points of the group early on can help you decide if you can handle the stress of the position. On the flip side, recognizing these issues might present opportunities for you to implement solutions, especially if you've previously encountered similar hurdles.

Chapter 12: Post Interview Actions

After the Interview

Once the interview is over, take some time to relax and decompress. Interviewing can be stressful regardless of how well it went. However, there are a few steps I recommended doing after an interview, since each interview should be used as a learning experience.

Personal Debrief and Make Adjustments

- **Next steps:** Hopefully the interviewer explained the next steps in the hiring process. If so, start preparing for the next stage. If it's filling out paperwork, make sure you complete it in a timely manner. If there's a second-round interview, start preparing for that.

- **Build your questions bank:** Immediately after the interview, write down the difficult questions the interviewer asked. Start creating a bank of questions you have faced previously and use them to practice for future interviews. Answer these questions when you're not under interview pressure, allowing yourself ample time to consider your responses. Try writing them out. If a question really has you stumped, try using other resources, such as a trusted friend, mentor, or even do an Internet search to see possible answers to the question.

- **Practice:** Continue to practice and prepare for the next interview, even if you do not have another interview coming up. Until you have an actual written offer in hand, you should continue to work on your interviewing skills so they are constantly improving. Even after landing a new job, take some time to maintain your interviewing skills. As stated earlier, every interaction is a type of interview. You never know who you will meet next or when you will need to interview for another job, position, or promotion.

- **Show gratitude:** Interviewing takes a lot of time and effort for both parties. An employer is dedicating their time and resources to interview applicants. It doesn't take much effort to show some appreciation that they took time to consider you for the position.

If at all possible, follow up with a short "Thank You" email to the interviewer. I usually like to wait a few days since it gives the interviewer time to finish interviewing other applicants, and the email serves as a reminder of you. Avoid being too generic with your email by including the following:

- **Name:** It's best to address a specific individual. This can be the recruiter or your interviewer. If you don't have the interviewer's contact information, you can mention their name in the email.

- **Personal touch:** Add something personal that occurred in the interview. The best thing you can use is their response to any of your questions. This shows you were listening to what they said to you.

- **Advice:** Always ask for advice any time you want to improve. You can and should ask for advice on improvement, especially if you weren't selected after an interview. I have personally emailed many recruiters and employees after an interview. For the ones where I didn't get the job, I would ask for advice on how I could be more competitive in the future. More often than not, I would receive some type of feedback. The best type of feedback was actionable— something I could work on. This helped me improve my own interviewing skills and discover my faults.

- **Social Media:** If you are in the process of applying for a position, be aware that your social media may come under scrutiny. If you use social media platforms, be mindful of what you post and with whom you associate. It takes only one bad post to tarnish your reputation, possibly leading to a missed opportunity.

  - **Don't announce too early:** Receiving a job offer is exciting news, you may want to exercise discretion on what information you reveal, to whom, and when. For example, you want your current employer to know ahead of time if you intend to leave the company. If you make big announcements on social media and your employer finds out such information through these channels, you will be in a very awkward position when you return to work.

  - **Avoid bad posts:** Always be mindful of your posts on social media. Any hateful, controversial, or unsavoury content should not have a place on your social media. I have seen offers rescinded based on an applicant's poor judgment in social media posts. Offers are sometimes conditional for reasons such as this. Even if you are passionate about a topic, before posting, take time to think about whether this is something you want everyone to see for a long time. Remember, once you post something to the internet, it is very hard, if not impossible, to remove all traces of it. You can find numerous examples of individuals who posted an offensive picture or controversial comment several years ago and are facing backlash and consequences years later.

- **Sanitize your network:** If you have acquaintances, friends, colleagues, or even family members that are prone to posting negative, offensive, or unsavoury content, your reputation may also be tainted solely by association. This is obviously up to your discretion. It's ultimately your choice, but I personally disassociate from those who regularly post offensive content, misinformation, or questionable posts that either I don't agree with or don't want to be associated with.

Offers and Negotiations

When I was interviewing for some of my first post-graduate jobs, I made the mistake of thinking a verbal offer was good enough. I realized my mistake after I had one of the best interviews with a partner of a consulting firm. He liked me so much that he offered me a position at the company and said that I would hear back from them regarding the next steps. I was excited and thrilled that I had landed my first job after college.

After a week passed, I was getting a little concerned, as I had heard nothing since the interview. I decided to call the company directly to find out what was going on. After some prodding and digging, I found out that funding had fallen through for the position. Since I had not formally signed any contract, there was very little I could do. I decided to call the partner who interviewed me and ask if there was anything else available at the company. Unfortunately, there was nothing he could do for me, and I later found out he had no authority to make the initial offer at the interview. I was upset, but I realized there really was nothing that could be done and I was wasting my time.

Remember, the offer is not yours until you have an actual written document specifying the terms of your employment. The same is true for any type of promise of pay, benefits, etc. If it is not in writing, it does not exist.

Also, pay attention to the nature of the offer. If it's conditional, then you must meet certain conditions in order for the offer to be valid. The company should explain all disqualifiers clearly. If you are unsure or the disqualifiers are unclear, make sure you speak with the recruiter or hiring manager to resolve any issues or concerns you may have. An example of these could be as simple as graduating from your undergrad program. Thus, if you fail to graduate, the company does not have to extend the offer to you since you didn't meet the criteria.

Negotiations

As a recruiter, I usually inquire about the applicant's expected salary at the beginning of the application process. The reason I ask this up front is to ensure I am able to meet or even exceed the applicant's asking salary. This ensures I do not waste either the applicant's or my time going through the application process if the applicant is going to be more likely to reject an offer in the end due to salary.

If you're the applicant, try to find out the salary range for the position before you apply or speak with a recruiter. This way, you can have a realistic number when asked the salary question. Give a salary range if you can, rather than a specific number. A range allows some flexibility or options to the recruiter. If you are asked to provide a specific number, give a number you would be comfortable with. If you're not sure what to pick or where to start, look at the industry average for what that position usually offers.

If your number seems to be on the higher end of the scale, be prepared to rationalize it. Take a holistic approach; weigh factors such as formal education, recognized certifications, the current industry average, the number of years with relevant job experience, the current job and the current salary (if it's related to the position you are applying for). If your current job is in the same field, then use it as base pay and calculate it up depending on the length of employment. If your current job is not in the same field, discern how your skills can be translated. You need to justify the amount you're asking.

Money Isn't Everything
After an offer is extended, you should look beyond the base salary. All too often, applicants turn down offers because they focus solely on the initial dollar amount. I recall one applicant who rejected an offer simply because another company offered him $5,000 more. However, a year later, he reapplied because the other company did not have a career path for his position and he realized he would be stuck at that salary for quite some time, whereas my company allowed for advancement. While an offer may sound great initially, if there is no room for growth or if it will not help you meet your career goals, you may need to reconsider.

Sometimes, employer benefits can outweigh the initial base salary offered by the company. Many applicants overlook these advantages if they don't ask the right questions or seek out this information. Insurance, student loan repayments, higher education/training, and retirement programs are just some of the other benefits to consider. Always look at the full package in regards to benefits and see what you need most. Some questions you may ask:

Do you have career advancement tracks? How do they work?

See how the company can help you reach your career aspirations. Find out what type of training or certifications they offer. See how the company can help you progress.

What kind of training do you support and/or provide?

Some companies may offer continuing education and training opportunities. These can be worth more than your salary since they help build your skills and knowledge.

How often do promotions/raises occur? Are there bonuses?

If the initial offer seems below your salary expectations, ask how the company promotes their employees or if they give bonuses. You may find that your salary requirement can be met in the end. However, if promotions are heavily influenced by office politics and you're not comfortable with that environment, you might want to think twice before committing.

Is there a sign on bonus? If so, what kind of obligations are involved?

I've seen applicants decline offers because they were bound to a company by service agreements or faced penalties for not fulfilling a signing bonus's conditions. If you're currently employed, be clear about any obligations you have before applying to another company.

Is this a salary position?

It's important to understand how you will be compensated. If you're salaried, you may be rewarded for working faster. The drawback is that you may be required to work longer hours during final product deliverables or releases.

If my overtime is billable, would I be compensated?

Some companies require their employees to work beyond the standard 9-5 hours. Find out what kind of compensation they offer for going beyond normal hours.

Do you have health, vision, and dental insurances? If so, can I have a copy of the insurance coverage?

Find out what kind of insurance you need and plan for the future. Even if you are a healthy, single, young adult, you never know what life changes may come your way and you may require different insurance.

What is the waiting period before my health insurance becomes effective?

When transitioning between jobs, ensure your insurance doesn't lapse. Some companies have a waiting period before insurance benefits kick in. If the company's coverage only starts after a year, are you able to arrange other coverage? Are you prepared for unexpected out-of-pocket medical expenses during any gaps?

What about retirement plans and company matching?

Many companies have a retirement plan of some sort. Take time to understand them. While this book won't delve deeply into retirement planning, it's crucial to start early in your career. One concept is employer matching contributions. For example, an employer may offer a 401(k) plan where you can make annual contributions; the maximum amount you can contribute is set by the IRS each year.

The company may offer to match a certain percentage of these contributions. A good practice is to invest at least the amount that the company matches. If the company will match 5% of your contributions, try to invest in at least 5%, since the company is essentially providing you with a risk-free return of 5% on your investment. Some companies may even have a higher matching percentage. Take time to understand the different types of funds and how aggressive or conservative you want to be in your investments. At the very least, come up with a retirement plan for yourself.

What is the vesting period for the company?

A vesting period is the minimum amount of time you must work for a company in order to own outright employer contributions to a retirement plan, shares of company stock, or employee stock options. If you are not looking to stay long term with an employer, this is something to consider prior to leaving.

Is there any program in place for equity purchase?

If you are applying for a company that is a start-up or is a company that may have growth in the future, exploring investment opportunities in the company might prove lucrative in the long run.

Can I have the Profit and Loss (P&L) statement of the company for the last three years?

Most likely, a company will not give this information, but gaining this information can give a unique perspective on how well the company is doing. If the company is losing money, they may not be around for much longer.

EMPLOYMENT

You've landed your dream job—congratulations!

Now that you were offered your dream job, and you're finally hired, what do you do?

With the start of any new position, it's time to get to work! To help you on your way, this section touches upon a few topics that will help you in moving forward in your career. While there's a plethora of other topics we could delve into, consider this as your starting point.

Chapter 13: The Path to a Career

Your Career

In my first full-time position after college, I struggled to transition my mindset from job culture to career culture, especially in terms of promotions. First, let me explain the difference between a job and a career. A job is a position where you work and are paid or compensated in some way. On the other hand, a career is a long-term endeavour that you work towards. One such measurement of career growth is promotion.

When my yearly review came up, I did very little to push for a promotion. I focused on learning how to do my job well and made sure I put forth my best effort, but I assumed this would be enough for me to move up in my career. When promotions were announced, I was disappointed to learn I did not advance while some of my colleagues, who did less work than I did, were promoted. Here are some things I wish my younger self had known:

- **Be responsible:** Throughout your career, there will be individuals willing to help you grow. But you cannot - and should not - rely solely on their assistance. Ultimately, you are responsible for putting in the effort, seeking the training/skills, and navigating the company culture or politics.

In my case, I should have been more proactive in finding out what it really takes to be promoted in the first year. My lack of attention to how the promotion process works and what criteria are measured in awarding them was the major reason I did not get promoted. No one was going to hold my hand. It was my responsibility to understand the process and work on it.

- **Focus on yourself:** Don't compare others' success with your own. After missing out on the promotion, I found myself comparing my efforts to those of my peers, feeling frustrated when some were promoted despite not doing a great job.

As I complained about my situation, a friend of mine gave me the best possible advice: "focus on yourself." I realized that I needed to figure out what I needed to do to improve instead of fixating on what others hadn't done. I took my friend's advice and focused on what I could do instead—after all, there is always room for improvement in some form. In my case, I didn't fully understand the promotion requirements and also needed to learn a bit about company culture in order to petition for my promotion.

- **Invest in yourself:** To move up in your career, you need to continue to work on your tradecraft and learn new skills. The last thing you want to do is become complacent at your job. When I mentor, I ask, "What do you want in your career?" This may take some time to think about, but look at where you want to go next in terms of short term and long-term goals.

    Once you know what that is, start learning what it takes to be in those positions. Some companies have career tracks. If this is what you want to do, understand what is required early on. Take training and find shadowing opportunities that will help you gain the skills for those positions in that career track. And if your aspirations lead you to another company, you still need to think about what steps you need to take to get there.

    o Does this position require any special certifications? If so, how do I obtain them?
    o For this position, are there any required skills or

experience I don't have yet? If so, where can I find these opportunities?
- Who do I know currently in this position? How did they get there?

- **Take risks:** A young man, who I will refer to as Luke, asked for advice on what job he should take. He explained that he wanted to go into the tech industry but currently had to make a choice between two opportunities. The first was an opportunity to work as an unpaid intern for a software company. The second was a paid job as a waiter. I advised Luke that if those were his only two choices and he wanted to have a technical career, it would be worthwhile to take the unpaid position at the software company.

I explained that, while unpaid, he would receive technical experience and training in the internship rather than zero opportunities as a waiter. In the end, Luke took the position as a waiter, as it was a sure thing. When I met him a few years later, he was still waiting tables and had not moved any closer toward a technical career.

You should look for opportunities to push your limits in your career. If you never go outside of your comfort zone or go beyond what you have previously done, you will never grow. You will also miss out on many learning opportunities. Volunteer for assignments you don't normally do or take a chance on applying for a position - such as a leadership role, if you have never been in one before. At the retirement party of a mentor, he confided that taking on the hard jobs and projects no one else wanted gave him the most success and growth in his career. Understand that not all risks will pay off, but you can always learn from them.

Avoid Bad Habits

There are quite a few trends that have gained attention through social media in recent years. Some individuals have claimed that these trends have helped them find new paths in their careers. There is no question that there are some employers who are poor at recognizing hard work or valuing their employees. However, even though the following trends are currently popular when addressing employer issues, turning them into habits can be detrimental to both your career and your growth as an individual.

Coasting
This has been around for ages, but social media has spotlighted this trend, coining new labels such as "quiet quitting" or "act-your-wage." Basically, it's doing the least amount of work possible at a job without getting fired. Doing the bare minimum will get you the bare minimum results for your career.

Another consideration is this: if you are doing the bare minimum in your current employment, how are you going to give your best effort when it truly matters? Practicing a bad habit like coasting or justifying the mentality of "quiet quitting" will only prove difficult to overcome later.

Regardless of the job, doing the bare minimum is something that should be avoided. Success on the job comes when you do your best. Your best efforts will eventually be recognized.

Often, promotions come when you prove you are doing work above your current level or are taking on more responsibilities. In one company I worked for, only those individuals who achieved an "exceeds expectations" rating on their performance review were considered for promotions. In another company, showing what they called "sustained performance" at a higher level would qualify you for promotion. Promotions and career advancement are never guaranteed in any organization, but going beyond what you are asked will improve your chances.

If you find that you are not satisfied with your current job, start thinking of ways to improve your situation. There is always a better way to do something, you just may not have thought of it yet. Get into the habit of going beyond what is assigned or expected of you and your employers will see your value. If not this one, then the next. In the meantime, you will have built the habit and discipline required to perform at the level expected for your future career.

Applying for Everything
This is when someone takes a shotgun approach to applying to as many jobs as possible. The idea behind this is to get the best offer possible or use offers to negotiate a higher salary at your current position. Remember, it takes time to go through the application process for any company. If you're blindly

applying to a whole slew of companies, then you're going to be wasting a lot of other people's time as well. Come up with a plan when applying for jobs and target the companies you actually want to work for.

If you're only applying to use it as a bargaining chip for more compensation at your current company, you're wasting a lot of time when you could have learned to develop your communications and negotiation skills to discuss matters directly with your current employer.

Job Hopping
As I mentioned earlier, resumes with too many short-term jobs can be a red flag for potential employers, raising concerns about your level of commitment. Employers want to know that they can count on you in both the good times and the tough times.

If you're unhappy with your current job and it has only been a few weeks or months, decide which issues are the ones you can deal with or learn to deal with and which ones you cannot before deciding to quit. The choice to leave a company should not be reactionary, but something that comes with thought, planning, and weighing your options.

Learn how to communicate with your manager if you feel you aren't being adequately compensated or if you want other types of work. If you are having difficulties communicating with your manager, talk it out with a trusted individual, like a mentor and see what options there are. However, if you find that quitting is the only way forward, I advise that you go by the one "hop" rule: if you must leave a position in less than a year, ensure that the next position or job you are in should be longer in order to dispel any notion of job hopping.

Excuses

When the Covid-19 pandemic hit, everyone had a difficult time. I have met numerous student applicants who used the pandemic as an excuse for poor grades or lack of experience. However, I have met others who took that time to independently learn new skills, found unique opportunities to gain experience, or innovated new ways to adjust to their situation. In a similar fashion, I have seen employees use their personal circumstances as an excuse to avoid work. We all face difficult circumstances or hardships throughout our lives. Regardless of your situation, never use it as an excuse.

Abusing Perks

A young woman, whom I will call Marie, worked for a company that was very liberal with their leave policy. Recognizing the challenges posed by the pandemic, the company realized their employees would have unforeseen issues that might require extended leave. Marie took time off for all sorts of things that were inevitably non-emergencies, ultimately being absent more than she was present. A couple months later, she was let go.

Work-life balance is important. Because of this, many employers offer flexible schedules and other types of perks.

Employers also understand there are legitimate times when you need to take leave to take care of personal matters. However, they also need to know they can count on you. In Marie's case, she overexploited her company's leniency. The available flexibility isn't an open invitation to be exploited without repercussions. Near the end of her time with the company, her employer could not count on her for anything. So, she was let go.

Not Working

Another issue I have seen is that individuals would rather not work than do something they would not like doing. I met a young woman who seemed brilliant beyond belief. She graduated high school at an early age and obtained a Ph.D. by her early twenties. She was currently unemployed, and asked me for advice on her resume. She explained that she wanted a position as an intelligence analyst.

However, her entire resume was filled with teaching experience and publications on topics that were not relevant to the intelligence community. I explained that it shouldn't be too hard for her to get a job as a professor since her resume clearly showed aptitude for it, and it would be a bit more difficult to find a position as an analyst since her experience was so different. To my surprise, I later learned she had an offer in hand to work as a professor but turned it down since she didn't want to work as one.

Sometimes we just need to work before we can find an opportunity in a position we truly love. Never stay unemployed by your own choice. Instead, seek to be productive, learn to work, and gain new skills. Treat current job offers as opportunities to make yourself competitive for the job you want. Remaining unemployed will not only not help you gain experience for your resume, but it will also make you unappealing to employers, making you less likely to obtain your dream job.

Even when the job we really want is available, there are no guarantees that it will be everything we hoped it would be. Understand that there is no perfect job. While you can love what you do overall, there will be things that come up that you don't like doing but need to get done as part of the job.

Mentoring

Mentors can assist you in your growth, both as an employee and as a person. They can provide advice and insight if you are having a difficult time figuring out where to go next in your career. Regardless of the reason, having a mentor is always beneficial. If your company doesn't have a formal mentoring program, find individuals who can serve as an unofficial mentor for you.

Especially if you are new to a company, the quicker you can find someone you can learn from, the faster you can learn best practices and excel in your new position. While a mentor does not necessarily need to work at the same company you do, it is helpful if they do since they will understand company politics, structure, and culture. Remember, it's also never too early or too late to find a mentor.

- **Mentor in your direct career track:** Having a mentor in your direct career track is essential to improving your tradecraft and understanding what is expected of you in that career. Especially if this individual is where you want to be someday, why not learn from someone who has already walked the path you want to? They can share advice on what kinds of projects will help you build your experience or what kinds of training you should take to enhance your skills.

- **Mentor outside your career track:** A mentor who is not in the same occupation or specialty as yourself can still be helpful as well. This individual will have an outside perspective on what you are currently doing and may have ideas that you have not yet considered.

- **Serve as a mentor:** There will be a time where you will be in a position where you have knowledge and experiences that can advise others on how they can improve or avoid mistakes you have made. Why not share this knowledge and serve as a mentor? It is never too early to serve as a mentor to someone, as long as your intentions are to help the other individual grow. As an added bonus, mentoring others will also help you grow.

Networking

A colleague of mine once said, "You're not working if you're not networking." Creating a professional network can be very useful in finding new opportunities. While networking can be challenging for introverts, if you ever want opportunities to come your way, I have found networking to be critical. Here are a few ideas to help you build your network.

- **Social gatherings:** Happy hours, team building activities, and company events are some ways to meet new people or get to know your coworkers in a different light. You don't need to partake in all of these events, but you should go to at least a few.

- **Cross-department projects:** If you are in a large organization, there may be opportunities to work with other departments on a project. These cross-departmental projects can lead to other opportunities, especially if the project goes well. As you find more opportunities to work with individuals that are outside your normal realm of operations, you'll naturally expand your network.

- **Clubs or social groups:** Joining a club or a group that has shared interests or hobbies is a great way to meet new people. For instance, when the mobile game Pokémon Go! was released, I started adding other players' numbers as I met other players in my neighborhood. The player list became so large that I ended up creating a WhatsApp group to connect with everyone. I organized a few get-togethers and eventually we got to know each other well. A few years later, one of the members was looking for work. Coincidentally, he was looking for work as a project manager and it just so happened that my company was looking to hire. After connecting him with the project management recruiter, he went through the applicant process and was eventually hired.

- **Service projects:** Volunteer efforts are excellent ways to meet other people and a great way to give back to your community. Find a cause you believe in and take time to serve others. In your efforts, you'll never know whom you will work with or whom you will meet.

Some job opportunities have come my way solely because I knew someone. Sometimes you may be in a position to help someone else. If that is the case, you should offer help freely, as you never know when that individual may have the opportunity to help you in turn.

A long time ago, I was offered a summer internship with a prestigious accounting firm but turned it down for a better opportunity. I was still on their email list and received a mass email from the on-campus recruiter. To my surprise, it was an apology email regarding complaints she received from other firms that her on-campus presence was putting undue pressure on students and making them feel uncomfortable. It was a sincere apologetic email, but one I thought was not necessary. I immediately wrote back to her and expressed that I did not feel any such pressure and appreciated her availability in answering all of my questions and working with me when I went through the interview process. She wrote back and thanked me for the kind words and wished me well in my endeavors.

About a year later, I had a friend who was looking for a job as an accountant, but he did not know where to start. I asked if he had ever considered the accounting firm that had previously offered me an internship. He expressed his interest in the company but was not sure where to start. When I found out the on-campus recruiter had not changed since I attended college, I told my friend that I would send her an email recommending him.

Even though I did not accept the position at the firm, I figured I made a good enough impression that it could only help. In the meantime, I advised him to make the effort to reach out to her as well. A few months later, my friend thanked me, as the recommendation did indeed help, and he was offered a full-time position with the firm.

Referrals

The saying "it's not what you know, but who you know" is sometimes very applicable when seeking employment. However, just because your contact is referring you to a position does not and should not guarantee you the job. To facilitate the effectiveness of a referral, you should work with your contact before applying and before being referred, especially if there is a formal referral process.

As the applicant (the referral):

- **Understand the position:** Your contact is going to refer you for and ensure your resume reflects the skills and qualifications required for the position.

- **Timing:** Align with your contact about when to send in an application or other paperwork. Understand deadlines and do not procrastinate.

As the Contact (the referrer):

- **Don't refer everyone:** Your reputation is at stake. Make sure you have first-hand knowledge of your referral's knowledge, skills, and abilities. If you don't, you run the risk that your referral may not be qualified for the position.

- **Don't get overly involved in the hiring process:** As a recruiter, I've had numerous referrers who would continuously interject themselves throughout the hiring process. This was especially evident when it was in regard to a family member. I had one individual that even wanted to sit in on an interview. To have an equitable, accurate, and fair evaluation of your referral, leave the process up to the recruiter. While a recommendation can help the individual you are referring to, any unwanted meddling can result in negative results. Allow your referral to earn that position based on their merits, which you have hopefully emphasized.

- **Review your referral's application and resume:** Take time to at least look over their resume to ensure they have highlighted relevant experience and skills for the position. I have had referrals submit resumes full of grammatical and spelling mistakes or resumes that are completely irrelevant to the position. Also, make sure your referral applies to the correct position you are referring them for.

Work Journals

Many companies have some type of yearly review or provide regular feedback on how you're doing. Some companies may even give you the opportunity to review projects or significant work you have done for the year and may require a listing of these accomplishments to help them decide if you should be promoted.

In other companies, you may need to have a conversation with your supervisor or manager to explain why you believe you are qualified for a promotion or the new position you want. Consistently maintaining a work journal can help you easily recall your accomplishments and streamline the process of drafting any required documentation. Also, good journals can help you revise your resume or prepare for future interviews.

Your work journal does not need to be extensively detailed. Some ideas for details that you can include are:

- **Title of project or accomplishment:** This just needs to be a short title that will help you recall what the project was called.

- **Basic information:** To help organize your projects, have information regarding the name of the company the project was for, your current position title at the time, and the duration of the project. Include:

    - Summary
    - Quantification
    - Impact

- **List of formal training and certifications:** Keep a record of any formal training or certifications you have completed. Make sure your relevant certifications for your occupation don't expire. Having a list of your certifications, continual education, and training can prove your skills are always up-to-date and current in your field.

- **List of contacts/references:** Throughout your career, you will meet with and work with different people. Take time to keep a record of the people you work with. Include information such as when you worked with them, what they specialize in, what projects you worked on together, and their contact information. This will help you build your network.

Concluding Remarks

During my junior year of college, one of my goals was to obtain a summer internship that was relevant to my major. Throughout the year, I spent a significant amount of time with the university's career service and a business writing professor working to improve my resume. Once my resume was ready, I prepared questions for employers I knew would be at one of my school's career fairs. My planning and preparation seemed to pay off: several companies invited me to interview. I was excited and nervous at the possibility of securing my first internship. Little did I know, landing the internship was harder than I expected.

Interview after interview, I either didn't hear back from the recruiter or would get a regret email. While I initially felt that I conducted myself well throughout the application process, I realized that I was obviously doing something wrong. I needed to make adjustments to my approach to interviews and perhaps the entire application process. For each failure, I started reaching out to those who interviewed me, thanked them for their time, and then asked for advice on how to improve. While not all of them responded, I did get feedback from a few. I made a conscious effort to apply any guidance I received.

To cement these lessons I learned, I would share my experiences with other classmates and tell my stories about what worked and what didn't. Taking this a step further, I made it a priority to attend as many mock interviews or resume review sessions as I could to see where I could improve. Afterwards, I would repeat the process of listening to any feedback, figuring out ways to apply it, and then sharing that with my peers.

Even though I was unable to land an internship that summer, I did seek out other opportunities to build relevant work experience. I was fortunate to find an opportunity as an independent contractor doing outsourced analysis work on health care data, and I continued working as a teaching assistant for a computer programming class.

When my senior year began, I was determined to land my first full-time job before I graduated. I made a plan on which companies to approach during the career fair and ensured my resume was updated and polished. Just as the previous year, I was again invited to several interviews. Except this time, I was even better prepared: I had more knowledge of the application process, had practiced my communication skills, and had prepared organized responses to anticipated questions. By the end, my efforts paid off. I had six companies contact me with offers, and I found myself in the fortunate circumstance of being able to choose which employer I wanted most.

An unexpected outcome of my experience was a continued desire to share the lessons I had learned on my journey to full-time employment. The numerous mistakes I made and the long process of discovering the best applicant practices, are what grew my drive to help others find success in their employment endeavors. Over the years of sharing my experiences and teaching others, I have learned one thing: everyone's path to employment is different, but having a plan is crucial for everyone. To summarize major points of this book:

1. Decide what types of employment you want and build your knowledge, skills, and experience to qualify yourself.

2. Write your "limited edition" resume for those positions.

3. Treat every interaction as a type of interview where you can prepare and practice.

4. Once employed, adopt good habits, build your network, and keep a work journal in order to work towards a career.

Remember, as with Alice and the Cheshire Cat, you won't be able to make the best decisions for your journey until you know where it is that you want to go in life. Decide now what your future career looks like, then use the knowledge in this book to achieve it. I wish you luck on your path from applicant to hired.

Acknowledgments

This book would not have been possible without the support and encouragement from my family, friends, mentors, educators, employers, and clients I have interacted with over the years. As much as I would like to recognize everyone who has helped make this book possible, I would like to mention a few individuals.

Dr. Bill Baker, thank you for everything you taught me in business communications, resume writing, interviewing, and presentation. Your lessons have not only helped me in my career, but also inspired many of the lessons in this book. Also, my sincere thanks to Reid Grawe for all your job seeking advice and encouragement when I was an applicant.

A special appreciation to Robert Hodges for giving me opportunities to teach the students at Virginia Tech. The ability to conduct resume writing workshops provided me with invaluable feedback and experience.

I would like to thank my editor, Sanjana Verma for her meticulous attention to detail. Also, my graphic designer and personal friend, Ether Ling, thank you for your creativity on designing an amazing cover for this book.

My sincere gratitude to a few other friends: Matthew Madsen, Suzie Bastian, and all my coworkers who have continually encouraged me throughout this journey.

Also, my father, Val Chu, for always being an example to me and teaching me the importance of hard work and always looking to do things a better way.

Finally, I am forever grateful for my wonderful wife, Sarah. You've always stood by me and encouraged me to finally complete this book.

About the Author

Jeff Chu has a passion for teaching effective resume writing and interviewing strategies, and has taught hundreds of individuals in obtaining employment in both the public and private sectors over the past 15 years. He has presented at various institutions and organizations, including Virginia Tech, National Society of High School Scholars, and the LDS Employment Center.

Jeff has served the federal government for over a decade and has held positions such as Cyber Analyst, Applications Developer, and Recruiter for various technical positions. Throughout his career, he has received more than 15 awards for exceptional service and accomplishments and has mentored numerous individuals, helping them enhance their careers. He holds a Masters from the University of Utah and a Bachelors from Brigham Young University, both in Information Systems.

When he's not working or teaching, Jeff enjoys tinkering with technology, playing video games, creating art, and, most importantly, spending time with his wife and son.

www.employmentplan.net

www.ingramcontent.com/pod-product-compliance
Lightning Source LLC
Chambersburg PA
CBHW011408070526
44586CB00021B/2576